Instructions Manual

Process Guide for Students for Interdisciplinary Work in Computer Science/Informatics

Assoc. Prof. Dr. Andreas Holzinger

http://hci4all.at
a.holzinger@hci4all.at

Institute for Information Systems and Computer Media (IICM)
Graz University of Technology

Research Unit HCI4MED, Institute of Med. Informatics (IMI)
Medical University Graz

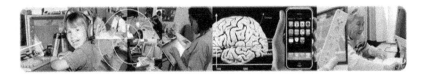

Data. Information. Knowledge. Decision. Action. This handbook provides some information for students with an interdisciplinary interest in Engineering (Computer Science), Natural Science (Cognitive Science/Psychology) and Business (Software Engineering Business). Human–Computer Interaction (HCI) and Usability Engineering (UE) can be seen as a bridge.

< This page intentionally left blank >

Anleitung – Handbuch
(Diese Arbeit ist in englischer Sprache verfasst)

Anleitung für Studierende zur interdisziplinären Arbeit in Informatik/Computerwissenschaft

Univ.-Doz. Ing. Mag. Mag. Dr. Andreas Holzinger

Institut für Informationssysteme und Computer Medien (IICM)
Technische Universität Graz

Forschungseinheit HCI4MED, Institut für Med. Informatik (IMI)
Medizinische Universität Graz

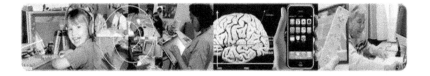

Daten. Information. Wissen. Entscheiden. Handeln. Eine Anleitung für Studierende mit interdisziplinärem Interesse in Ingenieurswissenschaft (Informatik), Naturwissenschaft (Psychologie), und Wirtschaft (Softwareentwicklung/Business). Human–Computer Interaction (HCI) & Usability Engineering (UE) kann als Brücke gesehen werden.

< Diese Seite ist mit Absicht freigelassen >

Abstract

The process of doing an academic work, whether a mini-project, diploma thesis, master's thesis or PhD thesis, requires systematic knowledge and skills in order to answer some of the following questions:

"How do I find a topic?", "How do I obtain funding money?", "How do I write a project proposal?", "How is the organisational workflow?", "How do I search Literature systematically?", "Why should I read patents?", "How can I organize my references?", "Why English as a working language?", "What is the formal structure of a thesis like?", „What is the classical hypothetic-deductive research process?", „Which research methods could I use?", "How will my posters, my presentations and my written work be graded?", "How do I contribute to a conference?", "How do I contribute to an archival Journal?".

These questions are discussed on the basis of Engineering (Computer Science/Informatics) and Natural Sciences (Psychology), which can be bridged by the subject "Human-Computer Interaction and Usability Engineering (HCI&UE)".

Since science is trans-cultural, inter-subjective and reproductive; these fundamentals can be further applied to almost any subject.

Keywords

Science, workflow, engineering, process model

Zusammenfassung

Die Durchführung einer akademischen Arbeit, ob Mini-Projekt, Diplomarbeit, Masterarbeit oder Doktorarbeit erfordert systematische Kenntnisse und Fertigkeiten um folgende Fragen zu beantworten:

„Wie finde ich ein Thema?", „Wie komme ich zu Förderungen?", „Wie verfasse ich einen Projektantrag?", „Wie läuft meine Arbeit organisatorisch ab?", „Wie führe ich eine systematische Literatursuche durch?", „Warum sollte ich Patente lesen?", Wie kann ich meine Literatur verwalten?", „Warum Englisch als Arbeitssprache?", „Wie ist der formale Aufbau meiner Arbeit?", „Wie läuft ein klassischer Forschungsprozess ab?", „Welche Forschungsmethoden gibt es?", „Wie werden meine Poster, Vorträge und schriftlichen Arbeiten beurteilt?", „Wie verfasse ich einen Konferenzbeitrag?", „Wie verfasse ich einen Beitrag zu einer wissenschaftlichen Zeitschrift?".

Diese Fragen werden exemplarisch an Hand von Ingenieurswissenschaften (Informatik) und Naturwissenschaften (Psychologie) besprochen, deren Brücke traditionell das Fach „Human–Computer Interaction und Usability Engineering (HCI&UE)" darstellt.
Da Wissenschaft transkulturell, intersubjektiv und reproduzierbar sein soll, lassen sich diese Prinzipien aber auch auf andere Gebiete übertragen.

Schlüsselwörter

Wissenschaft, Arbeitsprozess, Forschung, Vorgehensmodell

Table of Contents

1 Introduction and Motivation

1.1 Science

The aim of your work, e.g. your master's thesis[1] is to show that you are able to work scientifically. Science[2] can be defined as a *systematic* **knowledge finding process** and organisation of this "scientific body of knowledge" in laws and theories by observation, experiment, measurement, mathematics etc., aiming to be
1) inter-subjective,
2) trans-cultural and
3) replicable.

Note: If you are interested in Philosophy of Science (Wissenschaftstheorie) a good reader is e.g. (Chalmers, 2009).

1.2 Engineering

In an Engineering discipline, we want to *change* things, consequently you have to include the appropriate use of design and development methods, conceptual architectures and formal models, resulting in a working application. In Engineering you *apply* the gained knowledge from your scientific investigation (chapter 1.1) in order to
1) design,
2) develop and
3) implement applications, systems and processes that realize a requested objective and brings benefits for the end users.

---

[1] From Greek θέσις = position = intellectual proposition; the Latin equivalence is dissertātiō = discourse

[2] From Latin scientia = knowledge

1.3 Validation & Evaluation

Your applications are used by end users – your customers (!) – consequently a solid validation, verification and evaluation, and/or experimental examination is invaluable.

Validation is the process of checking if and to what extend your system meets the specifications and therefore fulfils (American English: fulfills) its intended purpose.

Verification is a quality control process that is used to evaluate whether and to what extend your system complies with official regulations, legal specifications, standards or norms.

Evaluation is the systematic assessment of your application by use of certain criteria against a defined set of standards.

Experimental Examination is testing the system against stated Hypotheses (e.g. "By use of the system A the task X is performed in shorter time than by use of system B") either in a laboratory or, better, in the field (real life experiment, field experiment).

1.4 Business Case

Along with your scientific and engineering contribution you should also present a business case (Geschäftsszenario), which is not to confuse with a business plan (Geschäftsplan). Your business case should demonstrate that your work contains merit, brings benefits to the end users, consequently *can* lead to commercial success. Example: You can increase the performance of your system; a business case would be to demonstrate that you are able to increase the performance of a workflow carried out by use of your system, so that you can show that your customer saves a particular amount of task time (= money), consequently the use of your system pays off. Note that time to perform a task is easy to measure, however, there are other aspects too, which pay off, including: quality, security, reliability etc.

1.5 Quality

While it is important that you enjoy your work, it must also be good high quality work and must reflect international standards. If your work is good, then this is good for your advisor. Therefore, your advisor want your work to be good.

The following pages can be used as a navigation aid for you, in order to steer your project work through the rough waters of reality.

I am looking forward to working with you.

Graz, August 2010, Andreas Holzinger

2 Abbreviations and Acronyms

ACM	Association of Computing Machinery, has a subject classification by capital letters and numbers, example H. = Information Systems, H.5. = Information Interfaces and Presentation (HCI), H.5.1 Multimedia Information Systems
A&HCI	Arts & Humanities Citation Index is a commercial citation index of over 1,100 of arts and humanities journals.
APA	American Psychological Association
CPCI-S	Conference Proceedings Citation Index- Science
ECTS	European Credit Transfer System (1 ECTS = 30 hours student workload)
EDA	Electro Dermal Activity (also Galvanic Skin Response, GSR)
EOG	Electro Oculo Graphy ("Blickbewegungsregistierung")
EPO	European Patent Office
GUID	Graphical User Interface Design
HCI	Human–Computer Interaction
IF	Impact Factor = measure reflecting the average number of citations to papers within a specific journal
INSPEC	Engineering Index especially for Physics, Computer & Control, Electrical Engineering & Electronics
IPC	International Patent Classification (Strassbourg)
OCG	Österreichische Computer Gesellschaft (Austrian Computer Society)
ÖSTAT	Austrian Statistics, or more precise ÖFOS which is the

Abbreviations

	Austrian Version of FOS (Fields of Science and Technology), example: 1108 = Informatics/Computer Science
PM	Person Month
SCI	Science Citation Index
SSCE	Science Citation Index Expanded
SSCI	Social Sciences Citation Index
UCD	User Centred Development
UE	Usability Engineering
USPTO	United States Patent and Trademark Office
UX	User Experience
UXR	User Experience Research
WG HCI&UE	Work Group Human–Computer Interaction & Usability Engineering (of OCG)
WIPO	World Intellectual Property Organization
WP	Work package
WTO	World Trade Organization

3 Organizational Procedure Overview

3.1 First contact

Talk to your advisor after his lecture or drop an e-Mail, ring him up and arrange a personal appointment.

3.2 Work types

Various types of work are possible, having various workloads, for example:

a) Mini-Project within the Lecture 706.046 AK HCI: Applying UCD, 5 ECTS;

b) Project Information Systems (Projekt Informationssysteme) LV 706.119, 10 ECTS;

c) Bachelor Thesis 15 ECTS;

d) Master Practical (Masterprojekt), LV 706.116, 15 ECTS;

c) Master Thesis (Diplomarbeit), 30 ECTS plus Seminar (Diplomandenseminar, LV 706.117), 5 ECTS;

d) PhD Thesis (Doktorarbeit – Dissertation).

3.3 Find your topic

How to find *your* topic is not an easy task. The only success factor is: it should *interest* you AND you should be *good* in it (see → **section 4**).

3.4 Literature research

If you have a specific topic in mind, take a look for the relevant background state of the art related work, which is constituted by publications and patents (→ **section 5**).

3.5   Find Funding

Money is an essential part for your research. There are some opportunities to get funding, either on a personal or a project basis (➔ **section 15**). However, whatever you are aiming for, you always need a *convincing proposal* what you want to do; see on how to write a proposal in (➔ **section 16**).

3.6   Initiate work

If you have found YOUR topic then you must:
a) for a Master's practical (15 ECTS) fill out the Student Work Proposal form;
b) for a Master's thesis (30 ECTS) the official "Anmeldung einer Masterarbeit"; or
c) provide a research proposal for doing a doctoral thesis (PhD); see ➔ **section 15** for how to write a proposal.

3.7   Formal structure

Write now (see section 4.4.) ! Do not hesitate!
Take the template from the student's help page http://hci4all.at/projects4students.html and follow the formal structure shown in ➔ **section 7**. Immediately start your work. For some help in English see ➔ **section 6**.

3.8   Research Methods

There are a lot of various research methods. Please remember that you will cover three areas: Science, Engineering, Business.
You find a basic introduction to the hypothetic-deductive research method in ➔ **section 8**. You find an overview on specific HCI&UE methods in ➔ **section 9**.

3.9   Courses

Along with your thesis you need to take the "Dipl.-Seminar" LV 706.117, Group Holzinger. Or you have to enrol to the Master's practical (see 3.2); Within these seminars you have to present your work at least three times (see sections 3.10 to 3.12 below).

3.10   First Presentation

After a few weeks after your start, you have to present your topic to your colleagues (→ **section 11**). The focus should be on aims, goals, objectives of your work, background and related work and the methods and materials you want or intend to use. You also submit the first pages of your work and on this basis you will get detailed professional feedback.

3.11   Grading criteria

An early important question is: on what criteria will your work be graded? (Beurteilungskriterien). You find them for poster in → **section 10**, for oral presentations in → **section 11**, and for written work in → **section 12**.

3.12   Midterm Review

At a progress report meeting, you present your work done so far. The direction will be checked, the progress tracked and future work discussed. You shall prepare a poster (→ **section 10)** and at least a conference paper (→ **section 13)** or even better a journal paper (→ **section 14).**

3.13   Final presentation

You present in a plenum and discuss your outcome. This is the finish phase and simultaneously a test run (Probegalopp) for your final exam.

3.14 TUGraz Specifics

As soon as you have done ALL your exams (Pflichtfächer, Wahlfächer und Freifächer) proceed to http://online.tugraz.at > "Prüfungsergebnisse" > "Abschlussprüfungen" > "Details". Here you assign ("zuweisen") all exams to the 4 blocks:
1) "Pflichtfach", 2) "Wahlfachkatalog 1", 3) "Wahlfachkatalog 2", and 4) "Freie Wahllehrveranstaltungen".
Attention, this button ("Abschlussprüfungen") does only exist after sending an e-Mail to the Dekanat asking for „Freischaltung für die Zuordnung". Note: You can do this from the very beginning of your Master study. Consequently, you have an excellent overview about your taken ECTS.
Attention with "freie Wahlfächer": here 1 semester hour counts as 1 ECTS, disregarding what the "Zeugnis" shows!

3.15 Formal check

If all "Zuordnungen" have been done – so far you have taken all necessary exams – you can click on "Freigabe durch die Fachabteilung". Now the Dekanat does a formal check and informs you in advance if something is missing.

3.16 Upload

You have to dispose the „Abschlussarbeit" in TUG Online. You need a German Abstract („Zusammenfassung") and a German title ("Deutscher Titel"). Attention: your thesis must be submitted in a certain Acrobat format (you can use the "help button").

3.17 Application for final exam

You have to schedule your final exam ("Diplomprüfung") at least 6 weeks in advance (minimum). The form is available on the webpage of the "Dekanat". You need the signature of your advisor (Betreuer) as the "Erstprüfer" and you have to bring the signatures of two further professors (which must be "habilitated").

3.18 Submission of your Thesis

During the Application you have to supply the following items:
a) One hard bound Master thesis (incl. signed statutory declaration (eidesstattliche Erklärung).
b) Application for final exam (Prüfungsanmeldung)
c) Optional: Blocking application (Sperrantrag), Attention: If out of the work a patent (even a small patent ("Gebrauchsmuster") could be gained, then this should be discussed during the early stage of the work, there is a form to fill out (Erfindungsmeldung), and remember: first patent, then publish!
d) Expert approval certificate (Gutachten) signed, original. Basically, this will be send from the Institute to the "Dekanat", however, please check ("kontrollieren, dahintersein".)
e) Application for the official graduation ceremony (Anmeldung zur Sponsionsfeier), optional. 4 weeks in advance (minimum) you have to pay the 7 EUR (as of August 2010) for your ceremonial diploma and to show the deposit receipt to the "Dekanat").

3.19 Examination

Please ensure to find a date where **all three examiners** are available. The examination consists of 30 minutes of presenting your work (including live demonstration), strictly following scientific standards (spartanic[3], no frills, no Schnick-Schnack).

After you have succeeded do not forget to celebrate – you have deserved it.

---

[3] From Greek Σπάρτα = Sparta, the city state in ancient Greece, synonymous for crude, but effective

4   How to find a Topic

Of course, you should choose a topic, which you find interesting, however, ensure that you are also *good* in this topic. There are some steps for a systematic topic finding process.

4.1   Active Reading

You should read *relevant* papers and conference proceedings and scan these for their **future outlook sections.** This should stimulate you *to think* and *to inspire* you. Within the conclusion and future outlook section, often the authors point out areas that need **further research.** That is a gold mine of ideas. If there is no such section, then ask yourself: "What *could be done* on the basis of this work?", "What *future directions* could arise from this work?" and "What *would you do* as the logical next step of this work?". The best way is to write a researcher's logbook and note what you have read and how the papers interconnect. From time to time review it. Provide a thematic clustering ($\rightarrow$ section 4.7).

4.2   Active Questioning

You should attend relevant lectures, talks, symposia, workshops, conferences – and most of all public final exams. Do not just sit there and listen. Ask! Formulate questions and stimulate debate. You can learn a lot from stating questions, however, you should always think first, then speak. Prepare your questions in advance. A good help was provided Benjamin Bloom (1913-1999) in his standard book (Bloom, 1956), which was the basis for a lot of other books. Bloom identified six levels of cognition:

1) Level 1: Knowledge, which Bloom classified as: remembering, memorizing, recognizing, recalling, identifying, duplicating, defining, reproducing etc.
Questions on this level are typically wh-questions: Who, What, When, Where, … "What was the core question of your research?"

2) Level 2: Comprehension, which Bloom classified as: interpreting, describing, explaining, indicating, reporting, reviewing, etc.

Questions on this level are typically retell-questions: "Can you describe your experimental setting in more detail?"

3) Level 3: Application, which Bloom classified as problem solving, application of information to gain results, use of rules and principles to alter something.

Questions on this level are typically How-Questions, e.g. "How did you apply the method X to gain the result Y?"

4) Level 4: Analysis, which Bloom classified as subdividing something to show how it is put together.

Questions on this level are typically Can-Questions, e.g. "Can you outline your results on what impact it could have for the application in X?", or "Can you show the benefits of your solution in contrast to Y?"

5) Level 5: Synthesis, which Bloom classified as creating a new, unique, original contribution or a combination of ideas to form something novel.

Questions on this level are typically What-for-Questions, e.g. "What solutions would you suggest to solve problem X?", or "What can we infer from your work for the impact in Y?"

6) Level 6: Evaluation, which Bloom classified as making value decisions about issues, resolving controversies or and the development of decisions.

Questions on this level are typically personal questions, e.g. "What criteria would you use to assess your application in X?", or "What is the most negative aspect of solution Y?"

4.3 Scouting

Read at least three papers per week from the most prominent journals of your field. Browse through patents within your area. Ask people what they would wish. Let them talk. Have your eyes open at all times. However, think that your aim is to finish your work in time, therefore be careful that you do not fall into procrastination. There is a common proverb by Voltaire (1694-1778): "The best is the enemy of the good" – whenever you try to be "perfect", there is the danger that you do nothing.

4.4 Stop Searching – Start Working

After a few weeks you must have finished your topic finding process. Start now – and using the words of Harold Thimbleby: **"Write now!"** and a good opportunity is to use the deadlines of conferences – and you kill two birds with one stone: you have some pages for your work and an internationally accepted peer reviewed paper. Even if your paper gets rejected, you get some feedback (Cairns & Cox, 2008).

Sometimes it is better to start with the number two topic, instead of waiting endless for your number one. If you still hesitate, note that the selected topic will not be the only research topic you ever will pursue, nor it will last for your life. In science new questions arise constantly; as long sought questions can become less interesting as new facts are discovered. Changing topics and areas can *stimulate thinking*. However, when you have selected *your* topic, commit yourself to it and go through it ("durchziehen") with all your strength and motivation.

4.5 Feasibility

Check, whether and to what extent a selected topic is a feasible area for you. "Do I have the necessary skills?", "Do I have access to the necessary environment, equipment, material I need?", "Do I have already some background in this topic?" (→ section 4.6).

4.6 SWOT-Analysis

SWOT is a strategic planning method *to evaluate* your **S**trengths, **W**eaknesses, **O**pportunities, and **T**hreats involved in your project to identify internal and external factors that are favourable and unfavourable to achieve your goal (see figure 1 and figure 2).

	Past and Present	Future
Positive	*S* *Strengths (Stärken)*	*O* *Opportunities (Chancen)*
Negative	*W* *Weaknesses (Schwächen)*	*T* *Threats (Gefahren)*

Figure 1 Basic SWOT Table

	Past and Present	Future
Positive	*What can I do really good?* *What am I proud of?* *What are my favourite subjects/projects?*	*What is the future chance of this work?* *What can I bring in this project?* *What would I be able to do?*
Negative	*What was particular difficult for me?* *What is my biggest weakness?* *What am I afraid most?*	*What are potential risks?* *What could I lose when doing this?* *What difficulties can I expect?*

Figure 2 SWOT Example

You can follow always these simple rules: set goals, develop strategies[4], evaluate strategies, monitor results and always gain commitment among all stakeholders (advisors, industrial partners).

---

[4] An important question is „What strategy do you apply?"

4.7   Thematic Clustering

From the viewpoint of HCI you can group and categorize various topics according to the following six categories:

1) SUBJECT (Domains, "Anwendungsgebiet")
2) HUMANS (End user groups, "Menschen")
3) CONTEXT (processes, "Kontext und Prozesse")
4) COMPUTER (devices, "Geräte und Maschinen")
5) INTERACTION (modalities, "Interaktion und Modalitäten[5]")
6) INNOVATION (changes in thinking, products, processes, ...)

4.7.1   According to Subject (domains)

The subject ("Fach, Anwendungsgebiet"), in HCI is called the domain (field of application) and is the target area in which end users apply your system:

a) Medicine and Health Care (Medizin und Gesundheitswesen): *e-Health, ...*

b) Education, Learning & Teaching (Bildung, Lehren & Lernen): *e-Education, e-Learning, e-Teaching, e-Didactics, e-Workplace, m-Learning, p-Learning, u-Learning, ...*

c) Business Applications (Geschäftsanwendungen): *e-Business, e-Commerce, e-Procurement, ...*

d) Governmental Applications (Öffentliche Anwendungen): *e-Government, e-Voting, ...*

---

[5] In HCI modality is a path of communication between the human and the computer (vision, touch, speech, etc.)

4.7.2 According to Humans (end user groups)

a) Patients, Medical Doctors, Nurses, Administrative Professionals, Hospital Managers, ...

b) Children, Elderly people, ...

c) Learners, Teachers, Tutors, Coaches, Administrative Professionals, School Managers, ...

d) Novices, Intermediates, Experts, ...

e) Able-bodied, Disabled, Impaired, ...

4.7.3 According to context (processes)

a) In the hospital, at the workplace, in the office, at home, at school, in the classroom, at University, in the car, in an aeroplane, outdoors, in the swimming pool, ...

b) Business, Pleasure, Leisure, Emergency, ...

c) Relaxed, wellness, well-being, feeling safe, secure, healthy, independent, creating new ways of User Experience, ...

d) Chaotic, hectic, stressful, complex, ...

4.7.4 According to Computer (devices)

a) Large screen devices, small screen devices, ...

b) Haptic touch devices, Multi-touch devices, Tablet-PCs (e.g. iPad), Smartphones (e.g iPhone), Handheld devices (e.g. iPod), ...

c) Mobile, wearable Computers, ubiquitous and pervasive, ambient devices, ...

d) Gameboys, Play consoles (e.g. Nintendo Wii + WiiMote,...), interactive Television (iTV), ...

4.7.5   According to Interaction (modalities)

a) Creativity, Inspiration, Thinking, Support, Aid, Tacit, Productivity, Decision Support, ...

b) Collaborative, Individual, Personal, Confidential, Passive, …

c) Security, Stability, Quality, Sustainability, ...

d) Speech, Gestures, Face recognition, Eye-Movement based, Smell, Haptical, Taste, ...

4.7.6   According to Innovation

a) Extreme Mobility, Hyper-Connectivity[6], Affective Computing, Perceptual Interfaces, ...

b) Multiple mixing & mashing, changes in thinking & learning, ...

c) Transdisciplinary (learning from other areas, import models from other disciplines), ...

d) Tangible Interfaces, non-WIMP Interfaces, context-aware interfaces, virtual and augmented reality (VR, AR).

---

[6] see Harper, R., Rodden, T., Rogers, Y. & Sellen, A. (2008) *Being Human: Human-Computer Interaction in the Year 2020.* Cambridge, Microsoft Research.

5 Systematic Literature Research

The literature is constituting the background and related work (sometimes called "body of knowledge" or "state of the art[7]") which include both publications and patents.

5.1 Publications

5.1.1 Categorization of Publications

Publications can be differentiated basically in five types:

A. Original articles in journals (Originalarbeiten in Zeitschriften);
B. Original contributions to edited books (Originäre Beiträge in Sammelbänden);
C. Edited books & edited issues of journals (Herausgegebene Sammelbände und Zeitschriften – special issues);
D. Original papers in conference Proceedings (Originäre Beiträge in Tagungsbänden, Tagungsbeiträge);
E. Authored student textbooks and Monographs (Lehrbücher und Monografien).

5.1.2 Science Citation Index (SCI)

An important criterion is: in which database is the publication listed. The basic rule is: everything which is listed in the Science Citation Index (SCI) is considered to have a good reputation; however, that does NOT mean that publications, which are not listed, are not any good. However, it also does not mean, that all publications, which are listed, are all good.

---

[7] "state of the art" is the highest known level of development of a field, device, method, etc

The SCI was produced by the Institute for Scientific Information (ISI) in 1960, now provided by Thomson Reuters and meanwhile covering 10,000+ journals from 256 categories and 110,000+ proceedings from the most significant conferences, symposia and workshops worldwide. The SCI is reachable via the so called "Web of Knowledge" (→ see figure 3) which can be accessed from the University Library pages, e.g. http://www.ub.tugraz.at

5.1.3 Other relevant databases via ub.tugraz

a) ACM Portal provides access to two databases, ACM Digital Library, which is the full-text repository of papers from publications that have been published, co-published, or co-marketed by ACM and other publishers; and the ACM Guide to Computing Literature, which is only a collection of bibliographic citations and abstracts.

b) IEEE Xplore is a broader research database that indexes, abstracts, and provides full text for articles and papers on computer science, electrical engineering and electronics.

c) INSPEC is a indexing database of scientific and technical literature, published by the Institution of Engineering and Technology (IET), and formerly by the (British) Institution of Electrical Engineers (IEE). The fields covered include physics, computing, mathematics, control and mechanical engineering.

d) Lecture Notes in Computer Science (LNCS) is the most important series of computer science books, published by Springer since 1973. It reports research results in computer science, especially in the form of proceedings, post-proceedings and research monographs. Two sub series are Lecture Notes in Artificial Intelligence (LNAI) and Lecture Notes in Bioinformatics (LNBI).

5.1.4 Search Procedure via Web of Knowledge

Do NOT use the Web for a literature research and I do not recommend to use Google Scholar. The best procedure for accessing full papers is to
a) Search within SCI Web of Knowledge (→ figure 3), and then
b) Retrieve the full texts via the Electronic Journals Library[8] (→ see figure 4). To retrieve the full document, you have to be logged on with your student's account and if not within the campus, you have to use a VPN client (see last paragraph).

Figure 3: The ISI Web of Knowledge – the first start for every research. The best way is to use the "Advanced Search" option, you can search by Field Tags (on the right).

---

[8] The "Elektronische Zeitschriftenbibliothek" is provided by the University of Regensburg, http://rzblx1.uni-regensburg.de/ezeit

You can now sort your results (→ figure 4) – amongst other options – according to:
1) relevance,
2) latest date (for example to see which is the most recent and which is the first publication!),
3) times cited (to see which is the most popular paper within the scientific community)

Figure 4: You can sort the papers found, for example, according to their "Times Cited".

You can read the abstract and decide whether you want to have a look on the full text of the paper. The simplest way is to download the full text via the electronic journal library "Elektronische Zeitschriften Bibliothek (EZB)" (→ see figure 5). For this purpose you need to know the name of the Journal (e.g. "Communications of the ACM"), the year (e.g. 2005), the volume (e.g. 48) the issue (e.g. 1) and the page numbers (e.g. 71-74).

Figure 5 The Electronic Library "Elektronische Zeitschriftenbibliothek" allows access to the full text (of course, only if the journal is licensed by the University Library).

Note: Check if you are sitting within the network of the University campus, because your IP-address will be checked. When working from outside you can install a VPN-client (CISCO) then you will be properly identified from anywhere, (see VPN: Secure Remote Access to TUGnet). Tunnels connect you from a separated network to the TUnet, so that your computer will become a logical part of the VPN server network (IP address from TUGnet: 129.27.*)[9]. Via the VPN client software you are able to connect to the VPN concentrator at TU Graz (129.27.200.1) at ports 500, 4500 and 10000 (UDP, TCP or IPsec).

---

[9] www.vpn.tugraz.at

5.2 Managing your References

5.2.1 Quality and Quantity of References

A look on the reference list provides a good estimation on the quality of the entire work. I require from my students that they know the **relevant related work of their field.** This includes the most important journal papers, conference papers as well as patents (see → **section 5.3**). Student textbooks (Lehrbücher), manuals or lexica should be avoided – this is commonly accepted knowledge and is not necessary to reference. The related work is essential, i.e. you should describe who else did which work on a – for your work – relevant topic. Example:

"A study performed by Reuss et al. (2004) showed that it is essential to obtain empirical insight into the work practices and context in which a mobile system will be used. They investigated the work of 14 physicians of a Swiss hospital with the patient record during their daily round and found that physicians have clear access preferences when they interact with the patient record during their daily round and a CPR system which is designed to ..."

Although quality must come before quantity, my personal proverb is: "a reference list is often too short ("Eine Literaturliste ist höchstens zu kurz"). Unfortunately, many authors do not a sufficient literature study, therefore do not really cover all related work.

5.2.2 URLs and Wikipedia

Please avoid URLs – whenever possible. It is annoying if the reader clicks on an URL and it appears as a broken link. When it is absolutely unavoidable to reference to a URL, please provide also the date of your last visit (e.g. last visited: 2010-08-14).

Generally, avoid any online sources (e.g. Wikipedia) – whenever possible: Rely only on solid archival literature which can be easily retrieved. Any paper having a volume number, issue number and page numbers, which is in a scientific database, and therefore can be retrieved is defined as an archived paper.

5.2.3 References: Quoting vs. Citing

In both Engineering and Natural sciences we mostly use references – rarely exact quotes (citations), as often used in the Arts (Geisteswissenschaften). You *reference* a paragraph of your work in order to reference the background literature or related work, thereby you *acknowledge* the source of your information or ideas within the text of your work. The only exception is, if you take out a piece of text from an author word-for-word, in order *to quote* the author's exact words to support your argument, you quote it (zitieren). Hence, we most often just reference (referenzieren) to related work. Example of a direct quotation:
It has been confirmed that *"Overall, previous experience with computers had a significant impact on the type of device that yielded the highest accuracy and speed performance (Wood et al. (2005), p. 419)"*.
The same just as a reference: Wood et al. (2005) confirmed in their experiments, that previous experience with computers had a significant impact on the type of device that yielded in highest accuracy and speed performance. References have another advantage: When referencing a source of information you are on the safe side. If the statement proves later to be wrong – then you are not to blame, you have properly referenced – the referenced authors did the mistake. Very helpful for you and your readers is a commented literature list (kommentierte Literaturliste). You not only provide the reference, you describe in a few own words, one or two sentences what the core essence of the paper is and what the main strengths, weaknesses and limitations are.

5.2.4 Reference Manager Software

A good reference manager soon pays off, because it not only stores all the references, it also organizes the appearances in the text and the style of the literature list. This might seem trivial to you, but it is annoying, e.g. if a paper is rejected and you have to reformat everything to another reference style (→ section 5.2.5). By using a reference manager this can be done by the press of a button. Some reference manager software includes:

a) EndNote. Along with MS Word EndNote[10] (→ figure 6) works pretty well and without any problems. Older versions also work very well and are much cheaper to get.

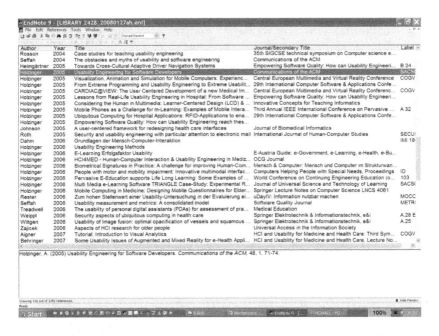

Figure 6: A look on a typical reference management software: EndNote.

---

[10] www.endnote.com

End Note for Windows creates a file with an .enl extension, along with a .data folder containing various MySQL files with *.myi and *.myd extensions. EndNote can be installed so that its features, for example Cite While You Write™ appears as a tool menu of Microsoft Word. EndNote can export citation libraries as txt, rtf, html or xml. EndNote has networking capabilities, and files can reside on a central server, but it does not support multi-user. There is also a version for Mac OS X.

b) Bibtex. Along with LATEX, Bibtex is the first choice. For example, JabRef can be used as a front end for Bibtex files. Bibtex uses a style-independent text based file format for lists of bibliography items, the file names end in .bib.

c) Sente. This is a reference manager for Mac OS X, which can search and retrieve any refs from sites supporting the Z39.50 or SRU (Search/Retrieve via URL) search protocols. Sente can be used to collect and manage related material, such as pdf files. Sente works well with Microsoft Word and Apple Pages.

d) Mendeley. This is a free desktop and web program for managing and sharing research papers, discovering research data and online collaboration amongst researchers. It combines Mendeley Desktop, a PDF and reference management application available for Windows, Mac and Linux with Mendeley Web, an online social network for researchers. The developers call itself the iTunes™ for research papers[11].

There are many other reference managers available, e.g. Papers, LiteRat, Zotero (Firefox Extension) etc. In case of doubt rely on tradition: EndNote, Bibtex or use an online tool such as Mendeley.

---

[11] www.mendeley.com

5.2.5   Reference Styles

A reference style is a set of rules for the handling of bibliographic items within a publication. There are hundreds of various styles in use, nearly every journal uses it's own style, so, a reference software tool pays off soon.

a) Harvard Style. I recommend to use Harvard Standard Style (Author, Year) within your work-in-progress as long as possible. This style is most used worldwide. The in-text citation looks like this (Holzinger, Kickmeier-Rust & Albert, 2008). The advantage is, that you can read the authors and year within the text (instead of looking always to the end of the document when having only numbers). The full reference to this journal reference in Harvard Style would be:

Holzinger, A., Kickmeier-Rust, M. & Albert, D. (2008) Dynamic Media in Computer Science Education; Content Complexity and Learning Performance: Is Less More? *Educational Technology & Society,* 11, 1, 279-290.

b) APA Style[12]. This is a slight variation to Harvard Style, the above shown in-text citation looks the same(Holzinger et al., 2008) (Holzinger, Kickmeier-Rust, & Albert, 2008), the full reference in APA 5th would be:

Holzinger, A., Kickmeier-Rust, M., & Albert, D. (2008). Dynamic Media in Computer Science Education; Content Complexity and Learning Performance: Is Less More? Educational Technology & Society, 11 (1), 279-290.

---

[12] http://apastyle.apa.org (there is the 6th Version available)

c) ACM Style. The same example in ACM Style would be in-text [1] and in the reference list it would appear like that:

[1]   Holzinger, A., Kickmeier-Rust, M. and Albert, D., *Dynamic Media in Computer Science Education; Content Complexity and Learning Performance: Is Less More?*, Educational Technology & Society, 11 (2008), 279-290.

d) LNCS Style. Springer Lecture Notes in Computer Science (LNCS) use a slightly different modification, the in-text looks the same [1], but the reference looks different:

1.   Holzinger, A., Kickmeier-Rust, M., Albert, D.: Dynamic Media in Computer Science Education; Content Complexity and Learning Performance: Is Less More? Educational Technology & Society, 11(1) (2008) 279-290

e) AMS Style. This is the style of the American Mathematical Society, the in-text citation is in square brackets [Holzinger et al., 2008] and the full reference looks as follows:

[Holzinger et al., 2008] Holzinger, A., Kickmeier-Rust, M. and Albert, D.: "Dynamic Media in Computer Science Education; Content Complexity and Learning Performance: Is Less More?" Educational Technology & Society, 11, (2008), 279-290.

Note: This is only a short introduction and the above shown examples are only for a journal reference, however, book sections, conference papers and other bibliographic items have a different appearance. You must refer to the style guidelines of your targeted journal, book series or conference. Do not mix up styles: if you use one style – use it consistently throughout your entire work.

5.3 Patents

5.3.1 Types of Intellectual Property

Intellectual property (IP) include copyrights, trademarks, patents, and industrial design patents (Gebrauchsmuster). Note: There are huge differences from country to country.

a) Copyright. Basically, this is the exclusive right granted to the author of an original work, including the right to copy, distribute and adapt the work. Attention: Copyright does *not* protect ideas, only their expression (referencing!). Copyrighted material principally needs permission from the copyright owner – who can license or permanently transfer this copyright to others (publishers). The German "Urheberrecht" for example is not the same as the anglo-american Copyright. The "Urheberrecht" automatically applies and cannot be transferred.

b) Trademark. Names, words, logos, symbols, designs, images etc. can be trademarked, i.e. they can be registered by the national patent office. The trademark (eingetragenes Warenzeichen) is designated by the following symbols:
TM for an unregistered trade mark, just to promote brands,

SM for an unregistered service mark, to promote or brand services,
® for a registered trademark (to protect the brand by law).
Within you work you are required to designate trademarks, at least the first time they appear, or you put an remark on the beginning (e.g. in form of a list).

c) Patent. The procedure, requirements and extent for granting a patent vary widely between countries according to national laws and international agreements.
Carefully determine between an Patent application and a granted patent (which is the result of the application process, most often

after many years). And have a look on economically successful patents (which are rare). The essence of a patent application are one or more **claims** defining the invention which must be:
1) new (original),
2) non-obvious (non trivial), and
3) useful and industrially applicable.
In many countries, certain areas are excluded from patents, such as business methods, mental acts, or software (→ section 5.3.2). The exclusive right granted to a patentee is the right to prevent others from making, using, selling, distributing, or exploiting the patented invention without permission.

5.3.2   Software Patents

Software based or computer implemented inventions are a matter of long debate. Some countries grant patents for all types of software, but in Europe this is extremely difficult and basically software (i.e. code, algorithms) are principally NOT patentable. Even if you mention that your invention has something to do with software the bureaucrats will immediately reject you.

Technizität. In German speaking countries there is much debate around the terminus "Technizität", which must be proven by the applicant: the developers must explicitly show that their invention actually makes a contribution in a technical field. In the US this is much easier because the rule is that it must be a solution for a technical problem.

5.3.3   Why should you read patents?

Patents along with Papers constitute the state of the art. If you want to cover the state of the art, or even want to go beyond state of the art then it is a must to know the relevant patents in your area. However, please take into consideration that especially software patents can be bogus and consequently a threat for progress. Illegitimate patent applications make their way through the US patent examination process without thorough review, especially in the software and web domain where state of the art is widely spread but poorly documented in archival literature. The result are trivial patents. Have a look at the Electronic Frontier Foundation: http://w2.eff.org/patent/wp.php

5.3.4 Patent requirements

Legal Requirements. Although there are huge differences amongst different countries, to call something patentable you have to proof that invention is: 1) novel, new, original (originär), 2) non-obvious, non trivial, and it must be 3) useful and industrially applicable (gewerblich nutzbar).

ad 1) Novelty. Novelty refers to the fact that it is not yet published anywhere – even the Web. Any publication in any medium immediately makes it non novel. The rule therefore is: First patent, then publish. In Europe, any publication anywhere prevents you from a patent.

ad 2) Non-obvious. This means that the invention is not trivial, however, this is a pure legal definition and not a scientific one. Finally, the patent examiner decides, consequently, the applicant can rebut the examiner's presumption through argument and written evidence.

ad 3) Utility. Finally, utility says that an invention must perform some function, be operable, and must be beneficial to society – this is exactly what HCI & UE is striving for.

Scientific requirements. A patent must contain a method AND a technical solution to go beyond state of the art. In some countries, certain subject areas are excluded from patents, for example business methods and pure mental acts (Gedankenmodelle).

Commercial requirements. A patent costs money (we are speaking about a range from approximately 10k EUR to 250k EUR), consequently the most important question is: Who pays for it? Therefore a market analysis is an absolute must. At least the costs for the patent should be gained – otherwise the patent is a failure (of which 90 % are).

US Kind Codes. Before January 2001 patents had the label A and patent applications the label B1, B2, ...; however, since January 2001, US Patents are labelled differently: A1 is the first patent application, A2 the second, etc., whereas B1, B2, ... are the granted patens! X-documents are problematic, because every X-document is detrimental for any further patent application in the area of the X-document!

Patent family. This is a set of patents from various countries to protect one single invention, when a first application in a country (priority patent) is extended to other offices.

Utility Patent. A lighter version of a patent is the utility patent (in German "Gebrauchsmuster").

Design Patent. Kind Code S is for the industrial design of a functional item, e.g. furniture, computer icons, etc.

Patent document parts. A patent consists always of:
1) First page showing title, abstract and patent information;
2) Detailed description of the invention, indicating how it is constructed, how it is used, and what benefits it brings compared with what already exists in this field (state of the art);

3) claims containing a clear and concise definition of what the inventors want to protect legally
4) Drawings.

5.3.5 Patent Search

Start your patent search via the European Patent Office (EPO) http://ep.espacenet.com/advancedSearch?locale=en_EP

Figure 7: Start by using the advanced search of the EPO

INPADOC Legal Status. It is important that you **at first** check the legal status of every patent, e.g. if the fees are not paid, the patent is void.

Sample Patent A. The example EP771280 (US5490072, DE69515118), Method and System for detecting the proper functioning of an ABS control unit utilizing dual programmed microprocessors, by (Hornback, 1996), shown in figure 8, is a good example for a patent granted.

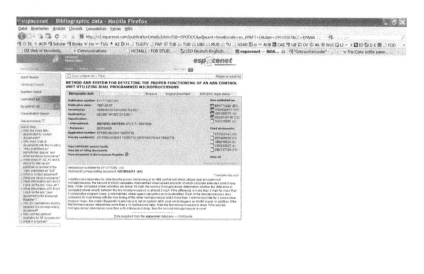

Figure 8: Example for a European Patent granted (Hornback, 1996)

Sample Patent B. The example EP1139245 (US5749785, WO9804991), *"A betting system and method",* applied by Sireau in October 2001 (see figure 8) is interesting: A quick look on the INPADOC legal status shows that the patent application has been refused in November 2003 – after exact 2 years of check (yes, bureaucracy takes a while).

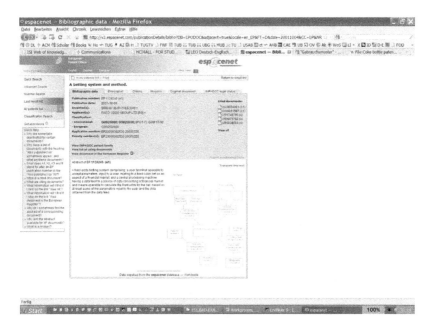

Figure 9 An example of a patent which has been refused after 2 years

Patent Rules. The EPO has updated their guidelines for Examination in one single document (597 pages) which is valid from April 2010 on and supersedes all previous rules. The rules can be downloaded for free in all three EPO languages (EN, DE, FR,) from the EPO website (last visited 15.8.2010):
www.epo.org/patents/law/legal-texts/guidelines.html
- The US Patent office is reachable via:
http://www.uspto.gov/
- The German Patent office is reachable via:
http://www.dpma.de
- The Austrian Patent office is reachable via:
http://www.patentamt.at

5.4 Publication Metrics

Since Universities must contract performance agreements with the government, publications in journals having high impact factors are important for ranking, benchmarking and finally for getting money. Moreover, a measurable research track record is also important for research proposals for getting grants.

Bibliometrics studies the measurement of texts and information by citation and content analysis in order to investigate the impact of a field, of a group of researchers, or the impact of a particular paper. In addition to simple statistics (number of papers, citations, etc.) the following metrics are popular:

Impact Factor. The IF was created by (Garfield, 1972), who is the founder of the Institute for Scientific Information (ISI) and the Science Citation Index (SCI). The IF is calculated yearly for journals included in ISI SCI, reflecting the average number of citations to the articles published. Related values include the
a) immediacy index (number of citations of articles in a journal receive divided by the number of articles published), .
b) cited half-life (median age of the articles that were cited in Journal Citation Reports each year), and
c) aggregate impact factor for a subject category (calculated taking into account the number of citations to all journals in the subject category and the number of articles from all the journals in the subject category).

Hirsch h-Index. Proposed by (Hirsch, 2005) this is a number based on a combination of your most cited papers with the number of citations which those have received. The index is often applied to measure the productivity of a group of scientists (department, university).
Note: The h-index does not consider the number of authors of a paper, consequently, it tends to favour subjects with large author

groups. The h-index is bounded by the total number of publications, this means that scientists with a few but groundbreaking discoveries are at an inherent disadvantage, regardless of the importance of their discoveries (Einstein's h-index would remain at approximately 4).

Individual h-index. Proposed by (Batista et al., 2006) the simple idea is to divide the standard h-index by the average number of authors in the articles that contribute to the h-index, in order to overcome the above mentioned effects of co-authorship.

Age-weighted citation rate. To further reduce the negative effects of the h-index the AWCR was introduced, which the average number of citations to an entire body of work, adjusted for the age of each individual paper.

Journal Citation Reports (JCR). This is a publication every year and provides information about journals (listed within the ISI SCI, including basic bibliographic information: publisher, title abbreviation, language, ISSN; subject categories (there are 171 categories in the sciences and 54 in the social sciences), e.g. COMPUTER SCIENCE; Basic citation data (# articles published during the year and # of times the articles in the journal were cited during the year by later articles in itself and other journals).
On this basis several measures are derived: the journal IF, the ratio of the number of citations to the previous 2 years of the journal divided by the number of articles in those years; the journal immediacy index, the number of citations that year to articles published the same year, the journal citing half life, the median age of the articles that were cited by the articles published in the journal that year etc. etc.

6 English as the Language of Science

Why English? English is the primary language of Science and is more strongly established than Greek in the ancient world, or Latin in mediaeval times (Garfield, 1989), (Jakob, 2008).

Scientific Writing. The main characteristic of scientific writing is clarity. Therefore it is regarded as difficult. Long sentences can confuse the reader. You should be short, precise and straight to the end ("kurz, knapp, klar").

Logical structure.
A scientific work, either a paper or a poster, has always the same logical structure. You can ask yourself the following 6 questions:
Question 1: "What problem was studied and why?"
Answer 1: Introduction and Motivation for Research section.
Question 2: "What was known before my study, and who carried out similar work?"
Answer 2: Background and related work section.
Question 3: "How did I solve the problem, what equipment did I use in which setting?"
Answer 3: Methods section.
Question 4: "What are the results of my study?"
Answer 4: Results section.
Question 5: "What do these results mean, what can we learn out of this work?"
Answer 5: Discussion and Lessons learned section.
Question 6: "What is the essence of the paper?"
Answer 6: Conclusion.

Abstract. This is a brief summary in order to quickly ascertain the purpose of the work at one glance in one single paragraph. It must not be an introduction.

Language Errors. German speakers recur often to the same language errors, some of them include:

Make. This is *not* the same as German "machen", e.g. "eine Erfahrung machen" = to have an experience; "einen Kurs machen" = to do an course; "eine Prüfung machen" = to take an exam; "eine Party machen" = to have / throw a party; "ein Foto machen" = to take a picture; EXCEPTION: to make a phone call ("einen Anruf tätigen"); to make an appointment ("einen Termin machen").

Singular/Plural. Experience = "Erfahrung (unzählbar)"; an experience = „Erlebnis"; experiences = „Erlebnisse"; people = Leute; peoples = Völker; work = „Arbeit (unzählbar)"; a work = „ein Werk", works = „Werke".

as ≠ like. He is a writer like a professional = "Er schreibt wie ein Profi"; He writes as a professional = "Er ist professioneller Schreiber"; Please do not use <like> as <similar>, e.g. the effect A is similar to the effect B (do not use like = "mögen").

proof ≠ prove (proof = "der Beweis", to prove = "beweisen")

rise ≠ raise. To rise (intransitive verb) = erhöhen, steigen z.B. our profits have risen this year.

big ≠ great ≠ large. Big and large describe concrete objects/people; great = "großartig"

bored ≠ boring. Bored = "gelangweilt"; boring = "langweilig" (I am boring = "ich bin langweilig ;-)

bring ≠ take. Bring me the book, but take me to the train station.

fit ≠ match ≠ suit. This processor fits into the casing ("passt"). This processor matches the requirements ("passt technisch"). This pocket computer suits me ("steht mir, passt zu mir").

hear ≠ listen. To listen to the radio. To hear a noise.

see ≠ watch. To watch Television. To see a customer.

False friends. Dangerous are words which are similar to German words, however, having a completely different meaning. Beware of:

to oversee = "beaufsichtigen – nicht: übersehen (overlook)"

to overhear = "zufällig mithören – nicht: überhören (to miss)"

to reclaim = "zurückverlangen – nicht: reklamieren (complain)"

to wonder = "sich fragen – nicht: sich wundern (surprised)"
adequate = "ausreichend, nicht: adäquat (appropriate)"

actual(ly) = „tatsächlich, nicht: aktuell (current)"

consequent(ly) = "daraus folgend, nicht: konsequent (consistent)"

decent = "angemessen, nicht: dezent (discreet, unobstrusive)"

eventual(ly) = "schließlich, nicht: eventuell (possibly)"

engaged = "verlobt, nicht: engagiert (dedicated)"

familiar = "vertraut mit, nicht: familiär (familial)"

genial = "freundlich, nicht: genial (ingenious, brilliant)"

massive = "enorm, nicht: massiv (compact)"

ordinary = "normal, nicht: ordinär (vulgar)"

plump = "rund(lich), nicht: plump (clumsy)"

pregnant = "schwanger, nicht: prägnant (concise)"

rentable = "(ver)mietbar, nicht: rentabel (lucrative)"

self conscious = "befangen, nicht: selbstbewusst (self confident)"

sympathetic = "mitfühlend, nicht: sympathisch (friendly, nice)"

thick = "zähflüssig, nicht: dick (corpulent)"

note = "Notiz, nicht: Note, Beurteilung (grade)"

promotion = "Beförderung, Werbung, nicht: Promotion (graduation)"

stuff = "Sache, nicht: Lehrstoff (material)"

bureau = "Amt, Behörde, nicht: Büro (office)"

chef = "Koch, nicht: Vorgesetzter (boss)"

concept = „Vorstellung, Idee, nicht: Konzept (draft)"

concurrence = "Übereinstimmung, nicht: Konkurrenz (competitor)"

to control = "steuern, nicht: kontrollieren (to check)"

direction = "Richtung, nicht: Direktion (directorate, head office)"

fabric = "Gewebestoff, nicht: Fabrik (factory)"

packet = "Verpackung, nicht: Paket (package, parcel)"

pause = "Unterbrechung, nicht: Pause (break)"

personal = "persönlich, nicht: Personal (personnel)"

physician = "Arzt, nicht: Physiker (Physicist) "

prospects = "Aussichten, nicht: Prospekte (leaflets)"

quote = "Zitat, nicht: Quote (contigent)"

For those who need some more guide on English the following Style Guide is highly recommendable :

The Chicago Manual of Style. The CMS is a style guide for American English published since 1906 by the University of Chicago Press. The sixteenth edition, released in August 2010 offers expanded recommendations for producing electronic publications, including web-based content and e-books.
Online: http://www.chicagomanualofstyle.org

7 Formal Structure of your Work

7.1 Formatting: no frills!

Format. First, a short word about formatting: NO SCHNICK-SCHNACK – no frills! Keep it simple. The content is relevant – not the wrapping.

Standard text. Times New Roman, 12 pt; Headers can be in a larger font (14 pt) and bold and – if you wish – in Arial.

Line spacing. 1 ½ ("Zeilenabstand").

Consistency. Whatever you do – do it consistently. Be consistent. Do not mix. If you make an error, and you do the error consistent, it is not so bad as switching always between two variants.

Backup. Under all circumstances produce more than one backup of your files and store them in different places. A crash is rare but can occur. A good solution is https://www.dropbox.com Dropbox functions as a web storage service with focus on synchronization and sharing. It supports revision history and the version control also helps users know the history of a file they may be currently working on, enabling more than one person to edit and re-post files without losing its previous form.

Filename. Always save your documents including your work acronym, name, date and initials within the filename, e.g. ACRONYM_NAME_20100306xy.doc
Please, do never send a file Diplomarbeit.doc ;-)

Statutory declaration. Do not forget the Statutory Declaration ("eidesstattliche Erklärung"). The standard text is as follows:

"I declare that I have authored this thesis independently, that I have not used other than the declared sources / resources, and that I have explicitly marked all material which has been quoted either literally or by content from the used sources".

Length. A word about the length of your thesis. Although an average Master's thesis has approximately 100 pages, there is no strict rule about the number of pages. Good theses sometimes have 70 pages and bad theses sometimes have 150 pages.

References. Refer to ➔ **section 5** Again: I require from my students that they know the most important related work of their field. This includes the most important patents, the most important journal papers and conference papers. These constitute the body of the state of the art of the related field, which everybody must know. For Reference Style and Reference Manager please refer also to ➔ **section 5.**

7.2   Word Processing Templates

On the webpage http://hci4all.at/projects4students.html you find **templates.** Basically there are two common recommendations (although there are a lot of alternatives of various word processors, I know):

a) MS Word. Although, there is a long debate about Word, it has – apart from many disadvantages – some advantages which are invaluable in academic work: Word allows change tracking, and exactly this is invaluable if you want rapid feedback; other people can easily provide feedback by just inserting or deleting text. Finally, Word is available in every bamboo hut. Word also works well with EndNote. You do not need a new version of Word. Word 2003 is well suited for task.

b) LATEX. If you use many mathematical expressions and formulas, then LATEX is surely the better choice – and it works well with Bibtex . However, collaboration on one document with more than one person is strenuous. It is, however, possible to use subversion and there are plaintext diff tools also available. However, be warned, subversion is ideal for software projects, however, not an ideal solution for collaboration on a few pages of text.

7.3 Protection from Plagiarism

Under no circumstances you are allowed to use any sources without acknowledgment to the source. And there is also a good aspect of referencing. If you express nonsense, and have referenced it neatly, then you are not to blame, because you did not say so – the authors who you have referenced did it. However, if there is nonsense and it is not referenced, than it is purely out of your mind and then you are to blame.

There are some online plagiarism detection systems available, here only a short selection:

Turnitin. This is a commercial plagiarism detection service created by iParadigms.
http://www.turnitin.com

eTBLAST. This is a non-commercial text similarity search engine, provided by the Virginia Bioinformatics Institute.
http://etblast.org

SafeAssign. Formerly known as MyDropbox (not to confuse with dropbox.com), this is a commercial tool
http://safeassign.com

TU Graz internal Service. There is an internal service available (Plagiatsdienst TU Graz) via: https://plagiat.tugraz.at

8   Classic Hypothetic-Deductive Approach

Developed by Sir Isaac Newton (1643-1726) during the late 17th century (but named at a later date by philosophers of science), the hypothetic-deductive method assumes that properly formed theories arise as generalizations from observable data that they are intended to explain.

These hypotheses, however, cannot be conclusively established until the consequences, that logically follow from them, are verified through additional observations and experiments. In conformity with the rationalism of René Descartes (1596-1650), the hypothetic-deductive method treats theory as a deductive system, in which particular empirical phenomena are explained by relating them back to general principles and definitions. This method abandons the Cartesian claim that those principles and definitions are self-evident and valid; it assumes that their validity is determined only by their consequences on previously unexplained phenomena or on actual scientific problems.

Basically, scientific methods include techniques for investigating phenomena with the aim of acquiring *new* knowledge, or *correcting* and *integrating previous knowledge,* i.e. going from state of the art to *beyond state of the art* (Cairns & Cox, 2008).

Question First. Every empirical research activity starts with a question, which should be relevant and interesting and should somehow be new, we say: original ("originär"). Consequently, at the very beginning, it is essential to search the relevant literature for the state of the art knowledge. In a best case scenario, contributions (called "papers") can be found, which are focused exactly in the area of interest. A closer look at the previous research in this area can uncover unexplored facets, inspiring the application of new parameters to provide NEW areas of discovery.

X vs. Y. During the formulation of the question, it is important that the correspondence between at least two variables is already expressed in this question. For example:
"How does variable x influence variable y?"
"What connection exists between x and y?"
"What effects are observable on x when altering y?"

Practical examples of different questions:
Literature survey: *What is known (and not yet known) to topic x?*
Feasibility study: *Is x possible ?*
Pilot Case, Demonstrator: *Is x an appropriate approach?*
Comparative study: *Is x better than y?*
Formal Model: *What underlying concepts does x have?*
Simulation: *What happens when I alter x?*

DV vs. IV. The basic idea is to define two variables:
1) a changeable or alterable (dependent) variable (DV), and
2) a unchanging (independent) variable (IV).

"How does y vary, when I modify x?"

Naturally, this can also be very complicated, e.g.: "in which relationship do the variables X, Y and Z stand to the variables U and W?"

A typical question would be for example: "a higher success in X is achieved by the employment of the application Y than the traditional method Z". Whereby, it is necessary to clearly define "higher success" and preferably using metrical expressions. "What you can not measure, you can not control" (DeMarco, 1982).

Experiment. Adopted from psychological research this is the Mercedes of empirical research methods. The building blocks of an experiment include:
a) Participants (please consider ethics);
b) Experimental Design (dependent and independent variables; within-subjects or between-subjects);
c) Materials and Methods (e.g. your software, your computer application, the methods which you use, see → section 10);
d) Procedure (formal description, of what your participants must do during the experiment, this should be inter-subjective, trans-cultural and repeatable);
e) Statistical Evaluation of the data;
f) Interpretation (lessons learned);
g) Conclusion (what is the core essence of your research).

Hypothesis. A working hypothesis (Arbeitshypothese) develops from the formulation of a question, e.g.: *"The learning success is greater with the use of the simulation X than with the traditional method Y"*. Again, using exact definitions of the terms used. According to the circumstances, the working hypothesis must be continually modified (see → section 9), until it represents, exactly what one wants to examine, e.g.: *"by the employment of the simulation X, learning time for the topic Y can be significantly shortened"*.
Here, a very careful clarification is necessary: Which variables are to be examined and which expectations exist (again with reference to the theory and/or to preceding work).

Formal scientific hypotheses (Popper, 2005) can be brought formally into the following form:

When X then Y; X implies Y; $X \rightarrow Y$

It is important to understand that *hypotheses are only conditional statements:* The effect occurs, not under all possible circumstances, but only under completely pre-determined circumstances. The hypothesis must be evaluated experimentally. Whereby there are exactly three possibilities:

1) TRUE. The hypothesis is significantly proved (verified = is true)

2) FALSE. The hypothesis is significantly disproved (falsified = is wrong)

3) UNDECIDED. The hypothesis can (on the basis of the existing data) neither be verified nor falsified (no statement can be made).

Note: Whether a hypothesis is true (thus ALWAYS applies), can not be confirmed due to the universality of the statement. Scientific hypotheses can therefore only be falsified. Nevertheless hypotheses can be differentiated with respect to the degree of their confirmation, whereby certain criteria is taken into account, such as how frequently and in which critical places the hypothesis has already been confirmed (Popper, 2005).

Experimental Design can be:
a) Prospective: Experiment / Quasi-experiment (= field study)
b) Retrospective: Ex-post-facto study

Formalization. Experimental designs must be formalized, in order to complete investigations according to uniform criteria (Sarris, 1992).

Definitions
EGr ... Experimental Group; CGr ... Control Group
TSn ... Test Subject n;
IV ... Independent Variable
DV ... Dependent Variable
The components of an experimental design are:

a) The groups taking part in the investigation (EGr and CGr);
b) The allocation or assignment of individual TSn to the EGr;
c) The experimental conditions (steps of IV) as well as the measurement of the DV;
d) The investigation sequence, thus the realization times of the IV as well as the measurement times of the DV;

Typical example: Pre-test post-test experimental control group design (Manstead & Semin, 1992):
Two randomized assigned groups are submitted to a pre-test. The EGr receives the *experimental condition (Treatment),* the CGr serves as a comparison control. At the end, both groups receive a post test.

This can be graphically represented as follows:

N O X O
N O   O

whereby

R = Random assignment (randomized)
N = Non random assignment; arbitrarily
O = Measurement of the IV, in the case of several Os in a line, always the same IV
Thus, for example, O1, O2... Measurement of IV1, IV2...
X = Treatment (no symbol is control group without treatment)
X1, X2, X3... several single factorial treatments
X11, X12, X21, X22... several treatments two factorial[13]

Operationalization. This is, in principle, the transfer from the theoretical construction to the observable measurement, e.g. from theoretical terms (actions), empirical (mathematical) variables must be produced. This is one of the most difficult aspects of scientific work; on which the result of the experiments is dependent (construct validity, see for example (Bortz & Döring, 2006)).

DV. The dependent variable is the variable, whose change due to the IV is measured (DV must measure the effect of the IV). The DV is described as dependent, because its developments are a function of the IV and therefore dependent on the IV. The DV should alter as a function of the IV. The DV is also referred to as a reaction variable (Sarris, 1992), since these practically represent the reactions of the VPn (e.g. the answers in the questionnaires).

CV. In addition, there are confounding variables (CV), which exercise unwanted influences on the DV (Bortz and Doering, 1995), (Christensen, 2001). The CVs are disturbances, because they also affect the DV, which results in ambiguity, causing variation in the DV on IV or the CV. Disturbing factors must be eliminated or at least controlled and/or sufficiently discussed within the paper (limitations of the study).

Experimental Plan. It is differentiated between pre-experimental plans and "genuine" trial plans. Pre-experimental trial plans are very controversial because they are very inaccurate and should therefore rarely be used:
1. Single investigation of a group   X O
2. Pre-test /Post-test single group plan   O X O
3. Statistical group comparison without previous measurement
                               N X O
                               N   O

The most important characteristic of a genuine experimental trial plan is the random allocation of the test subjects to the IV levels (Christensen, 2001).

1. Randomized control group allocation without pre-test

> R X O
> R   O

2. Randomized control group with pre-test

> R O X O
> R O   O

Power of Randomization. By use of random allocation of the test subjects to the groups (X = experimental group, blank space = control group), almost all interference factors are controlled, with the exception of socially based sources of error.

Of course, the random allocation of the TSn on the experimental groups cannot eliminate disruptive factors, but can keep them constant, with which the potential confounding variables work similarly in both groups, however the difference between the groups can only be backtracked to the IV.

There is still another possibility, quasi-experimental trial plans:
Pre-test/Post-test Control Group Design with *non-homogeneous* Control Group.

> N O X O
> N O   O

Simple time sequence trial plan

> O O O O X O O O O

Multiple time sequence trial plan

> N O O O O X O O O O
> N O O O O O O O O O

Arrangement with homogeneous time samples
$$X_1O \ X_0O \ X_1O \ X_0O$$
(X_1 =Experiment Condition, X_0 = Control Condition)

This trial plan ranks among the most well-known arrangements for the field of education because it is often simply not possible to take the VPs out of their environment and allocate them randomly to new groups.

Time sequence trial plans (Time-series designs)
With time sequence trial plans, the IV is measured several times before and after the implementation of the Treatments.

Simple time sequence trial plan
$$O \ O \ O \ O \ X \ O \ O \ O \ O$$

In contrast to the pre-experimental pre-test/post-test single group plan (O X O), this can control most disruptive factors.

Multiple time sequence trial plan
$$N \ O \ O \ O \ O \ X \ O \ O \ O \ O$$
$$N \ O \ O \ O \ O \ O \ O \ O \ O \ O$$

The multiple time sequence trial plan controls the interim occurrence by the inclusion of a control group and can be regarded, on the whole, as an extension and/or an improvement of the pre-test/post-test control group design with a non-homogeneous control group. In HCI research in particular, there are also other extremely interesting methods, which can be used successfully, especially in Usability Engineering, see in addition (Holzinger, 2005), (Holzinger, 2004). It is enthralling to combine classical research methods from psychology with the new methods from Usability Engineering and definitely provides much room for further work (see → **section 9**).

9   Quality Approach: PDCA Deming Wheel

This concept was developed by (Shewhart, 1958) as PDSA cycle. The roots can be tracked back to Aristotle (384–322 BC) and Francis Bacon (1561–1626). The PDSA cycle consists of four steps:
1) PLAN: Study the process;
2) DO: Make changes on a small scale;
3) STUDY: Observe the effects and
4) ACT: Identify what you can learn from your observation.

William E. Deming (1900–1993) promoted this model effectively and called it PDCA cycle (Deming, 1994) and is also known as Deming wheel:
1) PLAN: Clearly define the objectives and processes necessary to gain deliverables in accordance with the *expected output;*
2) DO: Implement the new processes on a *small scale* (e.g. within a trial or pilot project);
3) CHECK: Now *measure the outcome and compare* your results against the expected results and look for differences;
4) ACT: Finally, *analyze the differences* to determine their cause. Each finding can be used as input for a new PDCA cycle.

The PDCA wheel can be used to coordinate your continuous improvement. Every improvement starts with a goal and with a plan on how to achieve that goal, followed by action, measurement and comparison of the gained output. The most important issue is that you *act* – on a small scale – but act. Remember the "Write now!" approach in → section 4.4.

Deming introduced a "System of Profound Knowledge", consisting of four parts (Stepanovich, 2004):

1) *Understand* the processes;
2) *Know* the variation and the range and causes of variation and use of sampling in measurements;
3) *Find* concepts explaining knowledge and the limits of what can be known;
4) *Acquire* knowledge of concepts of human nature.

On the basis of Deming's "System of Profound Knowledge" the following competencies can be developed (Scholtes, 1999):

1) Ability to think in terms of *systems and processes;*
2) Ability to understand *variability* of all work;
3) Understanding for learning, developing and *improvement;*
4) Understanding people and their *behaviour;*
5) Understanding the *interaction* between systems and variations;
6) Providing vision, meaning, direction and *focus.*

The core essence of Deming's work was the sentence: "Without a purpose there is no system" and he provided the example of cleaning a table – where just looking on the process "cleaning" is not enough – you must know the *context:*

a) You can clean a table for repairing an engine;
b) You can clean a table for eating;
c) You can clean a table for a surgical operation.

Consequently, *"What is the purpose?"* is one of the most useful questions, which can be asked (Scholtes, 1999). However, you must do it, alter, e.g. make a device like its predecessor – only *better* (Thimbleby, 2007).

10 Research Methods in HCI

Whereas controlled experiments or at least quasi-experiments are the Mercedes of science (see → **section 8**), there are a lot of other methods available, which can be useful for your work.

10.1 Usability Inspection Methods

This is the name of a set of methods for identifying usability problems and improving the usability of a graphical user interface design (GUID) by checking against established standards (Holzinger, 2005). These include Heuristic Evaluation, Cognitive Walkthrough and Action Analysis (see → figure 10).

10.1.1 Heuristic[14] Evaluation (HE)

It involves having usability specialists judge whether each dialogue element follows established usability principles (Nielsen & Mack, 1994). The original approach is for each individual evaluator to inspect the interface alone. Only after all the evaluations have been completed are the evaluators allowed to communicate and aggregate their findings. This is important in order to ensure independent and unbiased evaluations. During a single evaluation session, the evaluator goes through the interface several times and inspects the various dialogue elements and compares them with a list of recognized usability principles (e.g. the Usability Heuristics by Nielsen (Nielsen, 1994)). There are different versions of HE currently available which for example have also a cooperative character. The heuristics to be used need to be carefully selected so that they reflect the specific system being inspected, this especially under the viewpoint of Web-based services where additional heuristics become increasingly

---

[14] from Greek Ευρίσκω for "discover" is used for experience based techniques

important. Usually 3 to 5 expert evaluators are necessary (cost factor), less experienced people can perform a HE, but the results are not as good. At the same time this version of HE is appropriate at times, depending on who is available to participate. Attention: HE does not necessarily result in evaluating the complete design since there is no mechanism to ensure the entire design is explored, evaluators can focus too much on one section or another; the validity of Nielsens guidelines has been questioned (Sears, 1997).

10.1.2   Cognitive Walkthrough (CW)

This is a task-oriented method with which the analyst explores the system functionalities, i.e. CW simulates step-by-step user behavior for a given task. The emphasis is put on cognitive theory, such as learnability, by analyzing the mental processes required of the users. This can be achieved during the design by making the repertory of available actions salient, providing an obvious way to undo actions and offering limited alternatives (Lewis & Wharton, 1997). The background is derived from *exploratory learning* principles. Several versions of CW exists including e.g. pluralistic walkthroughs wherein end users, software developers, and usability experts go through the system, discussing every single dialogue element.

10.1.3   Action Analysis

The method is divided into formal and back-of-envelope action analysis whereby, the emphasis is more on what the practitioners do than on what they *say* they do. The formal method requires close inspection of the action sequences, which a user performs to complete a task. This is also called **keystroke-level analysis** (Card, Moran & Newell, 1983). It involves breaking the task into individual actions such as move-mouse-to-menu or type-on the-keyboard and calculating the times needed to perform the action. The back-of-envelope analysis is less detailed and gives less precise results, however, it can be performed much faster. This involves a similar walkthrough of the actions a user will perform with regard to physical, cognitive and perceptual loading. To understand this thoroughly we have to keep in mind that goals are external tasks; we *achieve* goals; and tasks are those processes applied through some device in order to achieve the goals; we *perform* tasks. ACTIONS are tasks with no problem-solving and no internal control structure. We *do* actions. The main problem of task analysis (Carroll, 2002) is the difficulty in accommodating complicated tasks completed by more than one individual. Furthermore, the representation of a task analysis is complex, even when a simple task is studied and tends to become very unwieldy very rapidly. Such representations can often only be interpreted by those who conducted the analysis.

	Inspection Methods			Test Methods		
	Heuristic Evaluation	Cognitive Walkthrough	Action Analysis	Thinking Aloud	Field Observation	Question-naires
Applicably in Phase	all	all	Design	Design	Final Testing	all
Required Time	low	medium	high	high	medium	low
Needed Users	none	none	none	3+	20+	30+
Required Evaluators	3+	3+	1-2	1	1+	1
Required Equipment	low	low	low	high	medium	low
Required Expertise	medium	high	high	medium	high	low
Intrusive	no	no	no	yes	yes	no

Comparison of Usability Evaluation Techniques

Figure 10 Usability Inspection Methods versus Usability Test Methods (Holzinger, 2005)

10.2 Usability Test Methods

Testing with end users is the most fundamental usability method and is in some sense indispensable. It provides direct information about how people use our systems and their exact problems with a specific interface. There are several methods for testing usability, the most common being: Thinking Aloud, Field Observation, and Questionnaires (see → figure 10).

10.2.1 Thinking Aloud (THA)

It involves having a end user continuously thinking out loud while using the system (Nielsen, 1994),. By verbalizing their thoughts, the test users enable us to understand how they view the system, and this again makes it easier to identify the end users' major misconceptions. By showing how users interpret each individual interface item, THA facilitates a direct understanding of which parts of the dialogue cause the most problems. In THA the *time* is very important, since it is the working memory contents that are desired, thus retrospective reports are much less useful, since they rely on the users memory of what they has been thinking some time ago. A variant of THA is called *constructive interaction* and involves having two test users use a system together (co-discovery learning).

10.2.2 Field observation (FO)

Observation is the simplest of all methods and involves visiting one or more users in their workplaces. Notes must be taken as unobtrusively as possible to avoid interfering with their work. Noise and disturbance can also lead to false results. Ideally, the observer should be virtually invisible to ensure normal working conditions. Sometimes video is used to make the observation process less obtrusive, but it is rarely necessary. Observation focuses on major usability catastrophes that tend to be so glaring that they are obvious the first time they are observed and thus do not require repeated perusal of a recorded test session. Considering that the time needed to analyze a videotape is approximately 10 times that of a user test, the time is better spent testing more subjects or testing more iterations of the design. Video is, however, appropriate in some situations. For example, a complete record of a series of user tests can be used to perform formal impact analysis of usability problems. Another means of electronic observation is Data Logging, which involves statistics about the detailed use of a system. Data Logging can provide extensive timing data which is generally important in HCI. Normally, logging is used as a way to collect information about the field use of a system after release, but it can also be used as a supplementary method of collecting more detailed data during user testing. Typically, an interface log will contain statistics about the frequency with which each user has used each feature in the program and the frequency with which various events of interest (such as error messages) have occurred .

10.2.3 Questionnaires (Q)

Many aspects of usability can best be studied by querying the users. This is especially true for issues on the subjective satisfaction of the users and their possible anxieties, which are hard to measure objectively. Questionnaires are useful for studying how end users use the system and their preferred features but need some experience to design. It is an *indirect* method, since it does not study the actual user interface. It only collects the *opinions* of the users about the user interface. One cannot always take user statements at face value. Data about people's actual behavior should have precedence over people's claims of what they think they do. A still simpler form of questionnaire is the *Interview (I)*. The form of the interview can be adjusted to respond to the user and encourage elaboration.

Usability inspection needs to be combined with usability test methods. Some possibilities are: a cognitive walkthrough supplemented with a task independent method, such as heuristic evaluation. Indirect usability tests, such as questionnaires or interviews, must be supplemented with direct usability tests; thinking aloud or observation would be suitable. An absolute must is: Understanding the user's task, culture and capabilities; involving the users in the design early on; testing and iterating, with or without users.

10.3 Cognitive Modeling

This is an approximation of cognitive processes for the purpose of comprehension and prediction. The oldest approach is the Goals-Operators-Methods-Selection (GOMS) method (Card et al., 1983), which is based on the human information processing theory.

10.3.1 GOMS

This method is for examining individual components of user experience in terms of the time it takes to most efficiently complete a goal. Operators are the atomic-level actions that the user performs to reach a goal, such as motor actions, perceptions, cognitive processes etc. Methods in GOMS are procedures that include a series of operators and sub-goals. Selection, finally, refers to a end user personal decision about which method will work best in a particular situation in order to reach his goal.

10.3.2 KLM

The Keystroke-Level-Model is a restricted version of GOMS (Card, Moran & Newell, 1980).

10.4 Measuring the Human

There are many methods, here only a quick overview, for details see, e.g. (Wickens et al., 2004), (Rubin & Chisnell, 2008), (Cairns & Cox, 2008), (Lazar, Feng & Hochheiser, 2010).

10.4.1 Eyetracking

In German "Blickbewegungsregistrierung", it is the process of measuring gaze ("where do you look at") or just the relative eye movements by application of so called eye trackers. In contrast to the classical use of video cameras, there are methods available, based on Electrooculography (EOG), which consists of goggles with dry electrodes integrated into the frame and a small pocket-worn component for real-time EOG signal processing (Bulling, Roggen & Troester, 2008).

A recent example for research in collecting and analyzing combined eye movement and keystroke data from writers composing extended texts can be found in (Wengelin et al., 2009).

10.4.2 Electro dermal activity (EDA)

There are different termini in use, including Galvanic skin response (GSR), psychogalvanic reflex (PGR), electrodermal response (EDR), or skin conductance response (SCR). Basically, it is measuring the electrical resistance of the skin and can be used as a sensitive index of the activity of the sympathetic nervous system. Due to the lack of sensors that can be worn comfortably during normal daily activity and over extensive periods of time, research in this area is limited to laboratory settings or artificial clinical environments; based on this constraints (Poh, Swenson & Picard, 2010) have developed a novel, unobtrusive, wrist worn integrated sensor for long-term, continuous assessment of EDA outside of a laboratory setting. They evaluated the performance of this device against a Food and

Drug Administration (FDA) approved system for the measurement of EDA during physical, cognitive, as well as emotional stressors at both palmar and distal forearm sites.

10.4.3 Electrocardiography (ECG)

Cardiovascular data can be easily and non invasive measured and can be very helpful for usability research. A ECG basically is the interpretation of the electrical activity of the heart over time captured and externally recorded by skin electrodes. An interesting paper (Mandryk, Inkpen & Calvert, 2006) describes two experiments designed to test the efficacy of physiological measures when playing against a computer versus playing against a friend.

10.4.4 Further biological and physiological data

Basically, all human data can be used more or less for HCI and Usability research, including: Muscular tension (e.g. via a pressure sensor), respiration (chest contradiction and expansion), muscular positioning, and of course the vast area of brain activities (Electroencephalography, EEG). For a low cost solution you can have a look at (Stickel, Fink & Holzinger, 2007). A rough overview on these methods provide (Lazar et al., 2010), you can look at Table 13.1 (page 352).

10.4.5 Emotional Usability Testing

Emotion is an important mental and physiological state, influencing cognition, perception, learning, communication, decision making, etc. It is considered as a definitive important aspect of user experience (UX), although at least well developed and most of all lacking experimental evidence. Reliable emotion detection in usability tests will help to prevent negative emotions and attitudes in the final products (Stickel et al., 2009).

11 Data Analysis

11.1 Data Evaluation

A great deal of effort must be spent on careful evaluation, the assessment of differences etc. This is done with the help of inferential statistics procedures, see e.g. (Christensen, 2006).

MS Excel. This spreadsheet application is a basic tool, essential for all parts during research. It features calculation, graphing tools, pivot tables and a macro programming language (Visual Basic for Applications).

R. This is both a language and system for statistical computing and graphics, www.r-project.org and is open source. R provides many statistical (linear and nonlinear modelling, classical statistical tests, time-series analysis, classification, clustering, ...) and graphical techniques and is highly extensible. It runs on a wide variety of UNIX platforms and similar systems (including FreeBSD and Linux), Windows and MacOS. For computationally-intensive tasks, C, C++ and FORTRAN code can be linked and called at run time and one can write C code to manipulate R objects directly. The integration with Excel is provided by the RExcel package.

SPSS. Statistical Package for the Social Sciences, www.spss.com is one of the most used statistical software programs. This is a professional tool and accordingly expensive.

GraphPad InStat. This is a commercial scientific statistics software designed for statistical novices. It helps you pick an appropriate test by asking questions about the data. It presents results in simple paragraphs, with a minimum of statistical jargon.

11.2 Levels of measurement (scale types)

There are 4 measurement scales (Stevens, 1946) described:

a) **NOMINAL** (= categorical, e.g. arbitrary assignment of a code to an attribute, e.g. gender: 1 = male, 2 = female; statistics: mode, chi square; transformation: one-to-one = equality)

b) **ORDINAL** (e.g. rank grading, 1st, 2nd, 3rd, ...; statistics: median, percentile; transformation: order (monotonic increasing = order);

c) **INTERVAL** (e.g. Celsius-Temperature, equal distance between units, but no absolute zero point, 20° C, 30° C, 40° C, ...; statistics: mean, standard deviation, correlation, regression, ANOVA; transformation: positive linear = affine), and

d) **RATIO** (Kelvin-Temperature, age, wherever absolute zero point and therefore ratios are meaningful, e.g. 20 wpm, 40 wpm, 60 wpm [15]; all statistics of the above plus geometric mean, harmonic mean, coefficient of variation, logarithms; transformation: positive similar = multiplication = field).

Although this 4 level scales are very important and widely accepted, there is critic that it ignores important developments in data analysis over the last several decades. To follow this debate a good opportunity is to read (Velleman & Wilkinson, 1993). Further development was e.g. done by Georg Rasch (1901-1980), who developed the Rasch model, an example of the application of a Rasch analysis can be found in (Goh, Quek & Lee, 2010).

---

[15] Wpm = words per minute

11.3 Descriptive Statistics

To understand your data and to get a quick overview some basic statistical measures are useful: modus, median, mean, variance, range, standard deviation.

Modus. The mode "Modalwert" of a sample is the element, which occurs most often in a collection of data, e.g. from {1,4,7,7,7,8,9} the mode is 7. If your data is {1,1,7,8,9,9} the mode is not unique, it is **bimodal;** and {1,1,4,4,7,8,9,9} is **multimodal** and so on. Unlike mean and median, the mode makes sense for nominal data.

Median. This "Zentralwert" is the middle score in a set of data.

Mean. This is simply the arithmetic average.

Variance. It is used as one of several descriptors of a distribution and describes how far values are away from the mean.

Range. This "Spannweite" is the length of the smallest interval which contains all the data and is calculated by subtracting the smallest observation (min) from the greatest (max) and provides an indication of statistical dispersion.

Standard deviation. This is the square root of its variance and is used to measure the variability or dispersion.

This is just to mention some important terms of statistics and is by no means complete. Please refer to a standard students' textbook of statistics (Wu & Hamada, 2000), (Dalgaard, 2002), (Montgomery, 2008), and to your statistics course. A good online statistics course can be found here: http://onlinestatbook.com.

11.4 Comparing Means

In every user study you have multiple conditions or multiple groups and you are interested to find out whether and to what extent there is a difference between conditions or the groups. Here an example from (Lazar et al., 2010), p.75, on comparing the effectiveness of two search engines.

a) **Between-group design:** you recruit *two groups* of participants and let each group use one of the two search engines to complete a set of search task.

b) **Within-group design:** you recruit *only one group* and have each participant complete a set of tasks using both search engines. In either case you want to compare the performance measures of the two groups/conditions in order to find whether and to what extent there is a difference between the two search engines.

Note: Due to variances in your data, you should not directly compare the means and claim that a difference exists. Instead you have to use statistical significance tests to evaluate the variances. The significance test will suggest the probability of the observed difference occurring by chance (Zufall). If the probability $p(x)$ that the difference occurs by chance is low (e.g. less than 5 %) than you can claim with confidence that the observed difference is due to the difference in the controlled independent variables. However, there are various significance tests available according to the structure of your data, e.g. T-Test, ANOVA etc.

For a correct choice of the statistical significance tests, your question, the measurement scale, the experimental design and the resulting distribution of the data is relevant.

A result is called **statistically significant** if it is unlikely that the result occurred randomly. Hypothesis testing is done by using null-hypothesis testing, i.e., we assume that our Null hypothesis is true (no effect, no difference).

A decision tree of which test to use is available online [16] developed by (Blankenberger & Vorberg, 1998). Here only a quick guidance for you:

Exp. Design	IV	Cond. for IV	Suitable test
Between-group	1	2	Independent sample T-test
	1	3 or more	One-way ANOVA
	2 or more	2 or more	Factorial ANOVA
Within-group	1	2	Paired sample T-test
	1	3 or more	Repeated Measures ANOVA
	2 or more	2 or more	Repeated Measures ANOVA
Between- and within group	2 or more	2 or more	Split-plot ANOVA

Figure 11: A quick decision help according to (Lazar et al., 2010)

T-Test. This is a special case of analysis of variance for checking the significance of the mean difference of two (dependent or independent) groups. If the two groups which are compared are unrelated, then an independent sample T-test can be applied, however, if the two mean values are contributed by the same group, you better use a paired-sample T-test.
Lazar et al. provide an example:

---

[16] http://web.fu-berlin.de/biometrie/PDFs/Entscheidungsbaum%20Poster.pdf

a) Research task: You want to investigate whether and to what extent the use of a specific word-prediction software has an impact on typing speed.

b) Null-Hypothesis: "There is no significant difference in the task completion time between individuals who use the word-prediction software and those who do not use the software".

c) Recruit two groups: Let one group (= control group, e.g. 8 participants) type some defined text by using a standard word-processing software. Let the other group (= experimental group, e.g. also 8 participants) type the same text, but by using your word-prediction software. Note that you have randomly selected the group participants to provide that the groups are independent from each other.

d) Measure the time to complete the task for each group and put the data in a list, coded with group 1 and group 2, in our example:

C	0	0	0	0	0	0	0	0	1	1	1	1	1	1	1	1
t	245	236	321	212	267	334	287	259	246	213	265	189	201	197	289	224

*Figure 12 Sample data for independent-sample T-test
from the example of Lazar et al. (2010), p. 77
(C=Coding[17]; 1 = standard word processor, 2 = with prediction
software; ttpt = time to perform the task in seconds)*

f) Run an independent-sample T-test of the gathered data in figure 12. (e.g. http://graphpad.com/quickcalcs/ttest1.cfm)

g) T-Test returns a value, t, with larger t values suggesting higher probability of the Null-Hypothesis being false. The higher the T value, the more likely the two means are different.

h) 95 % confidence interval is used in significance tests

---

[17] The coding is dependent from the used statistical software, here: SPSS

i) Result: SPSS returns t = 2.169, which is higher as the t-value for the specific degree of freedom [18] (df=14, note that n − 1 degrees of freedom within each of the populations – this is an error in the Book of Lazar et al.) at the 95 % confidence interval.

j) Results from GraphPad: http://graphpad.com/quickcalcs

Two-tailed p- value = 0.0478 < 0,05

By conventional criteria (the 95 %), this difference is considered to be statistically significant.

Confidence interval

Mean of Group One minus Group Two = 42.13

95% confidence interval of this difference: From 0.47 to 83.78

t = 2.1688

df = 14

Standard error of difference = 19.423

Basic Statistics:

	Group One	Group Two
Mean	270.13	228.00
SD	41.85	35.59
SEM	14.80	12.58
N	8	8

k) Interpretation: *An independent sample T-test showed that there is a significant difference in the task completion time between the group who used the standard word-processing software and the group who used the prediction software (t(14)=2.169, p < 0.05).*

When you have two or more groups (e.g. a third group, using speech-based dictation), then you can use ANOVA.

---

[18] number of values that are free to vary

ANOVA. The analysis of variance (Varianzanalyse) is a collection of statistical models, in which the observed variance is partitioned into components due to different sources of variation. In its simplest form ANOVA provides a statistical test of whether or not the means of several groups are all equal, and therefore generalizes Student's two-sample t-test to more than two groups. ANOVAs are helpful because they possess a certain advantage over a two-sample t-test. Doing multiple two-sample t-tests would result in a largely increased chance of committing a type I error. For this reason, ANOVAs are good for three or more means. We extend our example, by a third group who uses speech-based dictation, coded as "2" (figure 13), the results shown in figure 14.

C	2	2	2	2	2	2	2	2
t	178	289	222	189	245	311	267	197

Figure 13 An extension of the experiment before,
according to (Lazar et al., 2010)

Data Summary	X_a	X_b	X_c	Total
n	8	8	8	24
sum	2161	1824	1898	5883
mean	270.125	228	237.25	245.125
sumsq	596001	424738	467054	1487793
SS	12260.875	8866	16753.5	45722.625
variance	1751.5536	1266.5714	2393.3571	1987.9402
st. dev.	41.8516	35.5889	48.9219	44.5863

Figure 14 The data summary by use of VassarStats
http://faculty.vassar.edu/lowry/ank3.html

ANOVA SUMMARY

Source	SS	df	MS	F	p
Treatment [between groups]	7842.25	2	3921.13	2.17	0.139102
Error	37880.375	21	1803.83		
Total	45722.625	23			

Tukey HSD test

Graph Maker

Figure 15 The ANOVA summary by VassarStats

The results from figure 15 can be reported as:
"A ony way ANOVA using task completion time as the dependent variable and group as the independent variable shows that there is no significant difference among the three conditions (F(2, 21) = 2,174, p = 0,139)".

ANCOVA. Analysis of covariance (ANCOVA) is a linear model with a continuous outcome variable (quantitative) and two or more predictor variables where at least one is continuous (quantitative) and at least one is categorical (qualitative). ANCOVA is a merger of ANOVA and regression for continuous variables, and tests whether certain factors have an effect on the outcome variable after removing the variance for which quantitative predictors (covariates) account.

MANOVA. Multivariate analysis of variance (MANOVA) is a generalized form of univariate ANOVA. It is used in cases where you have two or more dependent variables; and to identify whether changes in the independent variable(s) have significant effects on the dependent variables. MANOVA is also used to identify interactions among the dependent variables and among the independent variables.

For more elaborated information please refer to your statistics course or the literature recommended above.

12   Presenting your Work: Poster

12.1 What is a Poster?

A poster on a conference or workshop is a good opportunity for beginners to present their work in a more personal interaction with a scientific community, who are interested in your research. Basically, posters are very efficient, because they can be presented during the conference and afterwards act as a trophy in the home institute. Also, there is most often a "Best Poster Award" which is a good opportunity for young students and fits good into your curriculum vitae. Along with the Poster presentation most often a paper can be published within the conference proceedings. It is called poster paper and is usually shorter than a short paper, ranging from 2 to 4 pages.

12.2 What is the purpose of a Poster?

The purpose of a poster is to present work to an audience who is *walking through an exhibit area* during a conference (see figure 3), where the presenter usually stands next to the poster, allowing for passers-by to engage in one-to-one discussion. Back at home, posters are permanent stand-alone presentations for passers-by.
There are three main advantages of a poster presentation:
1) Mostly, only interested colleagues will come to your poster;
2) You get direct and personal feedback on your research;
3) You can generate contacts for further co-operations.

12.3 What is the structure of a Poster?

Posters are a special type of *presentation* and should neither be a paper, just printed on ISO A0 paper, nor a mounted set of various images. The poster has to orient an audience that is standing or walking around, and which is exposed to *distractions of noise* and *movement from other people.*

12.4 Poster size

The poster must never exceed the ISO A0 (84 cm x 118 cm = 841 x 1189 mm = 33.1 x 46.8 inches = 1 sqm) portrait format.

12.5 Designing a good Poster

Consider in advance the criteria on how a poster can be evaluated (see → section 12.8). A poster is a visual communication tool and should be an advertisement for you and your work ("Look, what I have done"). The text should strengthen the graphics in your poster. The most important text is the title – make it very obvious and attractive. The most common mistake in poster presentations is to use too small letters and figures. Design it that you literally allure your audience to your poster:

Catchy title 30-60 pt bold for a reading distance of 5 to 8 m
Authors 25 pt Bold reading distance: 5 – 6 m
Sub-titles 36 pt bold Reading distance: 2 – 3 m
Other text 5 24 pt normal reading distance: 1 m
Use simple fonts preferably sans serif (without feet) for both titles and text. Examples of useful fonts are: Arial, Tahoma, Verdana. Do not mix many different fonts. It is highly recommendable to use a lively self taken photo to show your own equipment, or the technology you have used.
Note: It should be possible to read – and understand – your poster in *less than five minutes*.

The poster message should be clear and understandable even without oral explanation, but not as dense as a paper. Be prepared for a 3 to 5 minute verbal explanation. People will likely ask you to provide a "poster walk-through", which you should be able to provide without reading any text.

12.6 Summary Handout

Prepare a summary handout, which can be, in the simplest case, just the poster in a miniature A4 format. This has two advantages: You can provide a "give-away" for your "visitors", and you can leave the handouts during you are absent.

12.7 Printing the Poster

You need a plotter, which is able to produce A0 sheets. If you do not have access to a plotter you can use a standard A4 printer and can print it in pieces. Adobe Acrobat can tile large pages, so it will print an A0 out onto 16 A4 pages: STRG + p > Advanced > tile all pages > (Layout, Pages per Sheet, Layout Direction). At the conference it is hectic, so it may be better that you produce a Power-Point Show consisting of 15 charts, which you can print and easy attach in a more sloppy order.

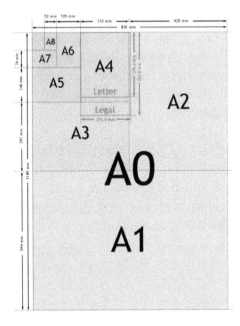

Figure 16: The ISO paper sizes (picture taken from Wikipedia)

12.8 Grading a poster

The grade for the presentation follows the Austrian 5-point-grading scale reaching from 0 to 100 points and ranges from very good (Sehr gut - 1 -) to failed (Nicht genügend - 5 -). See the criteria in section 11.8.

Fail	Poor	Average	Good	Very Good
Nicht genügend	Genügend	Befriedigend	Gut	Sehr gut
5	4	3	2	1
0-50	51-69	70-79	80-89	90-100

12.9 Criteria for the poster grading

1) PRESENTATION & STYLE (up to 20 points)
□ Provides the poster a "one-sentence-overview" on why one should have a look it and does it look attractive?
□ Is the poster well readable from a distance of 1.5 m?
□ Are the graphics in a good quality and well visible from the distance of 1.5 m?

2) INTRODUCTION AND MOTIVATION (up to 10 points)
□ Is the problem short, precise and well defined?
□ Is it visible, why this work is important?
□ Does it come out on how this work contributes to the scientific/engineering community?

3) BACKGROUND AND RELATED WORK[19] (up to 20 points)

☐ Does the poster – for this particular work – outline the necessary theoretical concepts?

☐ Does the poser contain at least three relevant related papers?

☐ Does the poster show clearly the state-of-the art?

4) METHODS AND MATERIALS (up to 20 points)

☐ Does the poster clearly describe the used methods and materials?

☐ Is the design and development process appropriately described?

☐ Are all used materials, equipment, devices appropriately shown?

5) RESULTS, LESSONS LEARNED, DISCUSSION (up to 20 points)

☐ Are the results adequately presented and interpreted?

☐ Are all tables, graphics and charts well related and well presented?

☐ Does the poster show the contribution towards beyond-state-of-the art?

6) BUSINESS CASE AND FUTURE OUTLOOK (up to 10 points)

☐ Does the poster include a relevant business case?

☐ Does the poster show any industrial implications?

☐ Can the presented work be used as a basis for a future work?

---

[19] The background constitutes the necessary theories, concepts and fundamentals - The related work constitutes current work that relates to your topic – state of the art

13 Presenting your work: Talk

13.1 Progress presentation

During your master thesis seminar (Diplomandenseminar) or your master practical you present the progress of your work 3 times:
1) The first presentation is at the very beginning, about the problem, the background and related work and possible solutions.
2) The second presentation is during your work and is a report on your progress.
3) The third presentation is a trial run (Probegalopp) before your real final exam.

13.2 Grading a presentation

The grade for the presentation follows the Austrian 5-point-grading scale and ranges from very good (Sehr gut - 1 -) to failed (Nicht genügend - 5 -).

Fail	Poor	Average	Good	Very Good
Nicht genügend	Genügend	Befriedigend	Gut	Sehr gut
5	4	3	2	1
0-50	51-69	70-79	80-89	90-100

13.3 Criteria for the presentation

0) FORMAL CRITERIA CHECKLIST (every point must be completed)
☐ Is the presentation template correct (black fonts on white background, without any frills)?
☐ Are the slides numbered?

☐ Is the amount of slides appropriate for 30 minutes (it depends on the topic)?
☐ Does the presentation include a reference list at the end?
☐ Are all figures readable?
☐ Are all references correct?
☐ Is the work well written and proofread (spelling, grammar, logical sentences, readability)?

1) PRESENTATION & STYLE (up to 10 points)
☐ Does the speaker present themselves well?

2) INTRODUCTION AND MOTIVATION (up to 10 points)
☐ Does the speaker present the definition of the problem well?
☐ Does the speaker express clearly why this work is important?
☐ Does it come out on how this work contributes to the scientific/engineering community?

3) BACKGROUND (up to 10 points)
(The background constitutes the theories, concepts, fundamentals)
☐ Does the speaker present relevant background?
☐ Does the speaker – for this particular work – outline the necessary theoretical concepts?

4) RELATED WORK (up to 10 points)
(The related work constitutes current work that relates to your topic – state of the art)
☐ Does the speaker present at least three relevant related papers?
☐ Does the speaker clearly outline the state-of-the art?
☐ Did the speaker mention to have checked relevant patents?

5) METHODS AND MATERIALS (up to 10 points)
☐ Does the speaker clearly describe the methods and materials?
☐ Is the design and development process appropriately described?

☐ Are all used materials, equipment, devices appropriately shown?

6) RESULTS (up to 10 points)
☐ Are the results adequately presented?
☐ Are the statistics correct and relevant for the work?
☐ Are all tables, graphics and charts well related?

7) LESSONS LEARNED (up to 10 points)
☐ Are the results adequately interpreted?
☐ Are the lessons learned well presented?
☐ Does the speaker clearly mention the contribution towards beyond-state-of-the art?

8) BUSINESS CASE (up to 10 points)
☐ Does the speaker show a relevant business case?
☐ Does the speaker mention any industrial implications?

9) CONCLUSION AND FUTURE OUTLOOK (up to 10 points)
☐ Is the conclusion a careful summary of the main outcome of the work?
☐ Is future work clearly described?
☐ Can the presented work be used as a basis for a future work?
☐ Are there outlines visible for future work?

10) DISCUSSION (up to 10 points)
☐ Can the speaker deal with specific questions?
☐ Can the speaker deal with questions that have not been anticipated?
☐ Would the speaker survive during an international conference?

14 Presenting your work: Writing

14.1 Grading for written work

The grade for the written work follows also the Austrian 5-point-grading scale and ranges from very good (Sehr gut - 1 -) to fail (Nicht genügend - 5 -). I apply a 100 point scale, whereby

Fail	Poor	Average	Good	Very Good
Nicht genügend	Genügend	Befriedigend	Gut	Sehr gut
5	4	3	2	1
0-50	51-69	70-79	80-89	90-100

14.2 Criteria for written work

For each criteria you get up to 10 points, with exception of the formal criteria, which must be fulfilled and any missing part will result in a "not accepted".
The criteria are categorized:

0) FORMAL CRITERIA CHECKLIST
(every point must be completed before submission)
☐ Is the cover sheet correct?
☐ Is the title ok?
☐ Is the abstract and the "deutsche Zusammenfassung" ok?
☐ Are the keywords and the ACM classifications correct?
☐ Is the statutory declaration „Eidestattliche Erklärung" signed?
☐ Is the list of abbreviations and acronyms complete?
☐ Is the table of contents complete?
☐ Is the formal structure ok (margins, page numbers, line spacing, Times New Roman 12 pt)?

☐ Are all page breaks correct?
☐ Are all figures readable, correctly aligned and described with figure captions?
☐ Are all references correct?
☐ Is the work well written and proofread (spelling, grammar, logical sentences, readability)?

1) ABSTRACT (up to 10 points)
☐ Does the abstract concisely describe the purpose, goal, and/or objective of the work?
☐ Does the abstract express the motivation for this work?
☐ Does the abstract describe the methods and materials used?
☐ Does the abstract concisely describe what the work contributes/adds to the scientific body of knowledge?
☐ Does the abstract stimulate an expert to read further?

2) INTRODUCTION AND MOTIVATION (up to 10 points)
☐ Is the problem well defined?
☐ Is it clearly described why this work is important?
☐ Is it clearly described how this work contributes to the scientific/engineering community?

3) BACKGROUND (up to 10 points)
(The background constitutes the theories, concepts, fundamentals)
☐ Is the background work described relevant to your work?
☐ Does the background work accurately describe the necessary foundation for your work?
☐ Is the necessary theoretical background sufficiently described?
☐ Are the – for this particular work – necessary theoretical concepts described?

4) RELATED WORK (up to 10 points)
(The related work constitutes current work that relates to your topic – state of the art)

☐ Is the relevant related work described and commented?
☐ Is the state-of-the art clearly visible?
☐ Have relevant patents been considered?

5) METHODS AND MATERIALS (up to 10 points)
☐ Are the methods and materials appropriately described?
☐ Is the design and development process appropriately described?
☐ Are all used materials, equipment, devices appropriately listed and described?

6) RESULTS (up to 10 points)
☐ Are the results adequately presented?
☐ Are the statistics correct and relevant for your work?
☐ Are all tables, graphics and charts well related to your work?

7) DISCUSSION AND LESSONS LEARNED (up to 10 points)
☐ Are the results adequately interpreted?
☐ Are the lessons learned well presented?
☐ Is a clear contribution towards beyond-state-of the art visible?

8) BUSINESS CASE (up to 10 points)
☐ Is there a business case for your work?
☐ Are there industrial implications resulting from your work?

9) CONCLUSION (up to 10 points)
☐ Is the conclusion a careful summary of the main outcome of the work?

10) FUTURE OUTLOOK (up to 10 points)
(Each work should form the basis for future and continuing work)
☐ Is future work clearly described?
☐ Can your completed work be used as a basis for a future work?
☐ Have you outlined your plans for future work?

15   Target: Conferences

15.1 Definition of a conference

A conference is an event in order to present and exchange work amongst professionals (researchers, scientists, industrial professionals etc.). Generally, the work is presented in form of a full paper presentation, short paper presentation, poster presentation, panel contribution, workshop contribution etc. usually within a slot of a session. The slot of a session typically is 15 to 20 minutes talk + 5 to 10 minutes discussion (20 minutes short to 30 minutes long presentation, or sometimes shorter or longer), whereas also a short time for speaker change must be considered. The slot is moderated by a session chair, who is responsible for the timing and deals with questions from the audience. The conference organizers are setting up the venue and provide the technical environment.

15.2 Peer reviews

The scientific committee ensures the quality of the submissions. They check the papers mostly in a double-blind review with at least 3 referees. Conferences having high rejection rates are usually considered having higher quality (however it depends). The quality of the reviews depends highly on the reviewer and can vary from very useful to useless and insulting (Wynn, 2001).

15.3 Types of conferences

A conference is usually a larger event (more than 100 people), whereas smaller events are called: Workshops, Meetings, or Symposia. They can range from a single track – single session to multiple tracks, having several parallel sessions with speakers in separate rooms speaking at the same time.

15.4 Conference Proceedings

This are the printed and published "books" available at the conference and forming archival (=reference able literature), i.e. they must have at least a ISBN and must be accessible via databases (SCI Proceedings, ACM Database, IEEE Computer Digital Library, etc.).

15.5 Call for Papers

A CfP is the official method for collecting papers, showing the important dates:

1) Deadline for submissions (usually full papers)
2) Extended deadline for submissions (short papers, posters)
3) Notification of authors
4) Early-Bird registration deadline
5) Deadline for camera-ready submission
6) Late-Registration deadline

15.6 Conference Announcements

The Cfp's are usually distributed via mailing lists or conference calendars.

15.6.1 Sample mailing lists

ACM SIGCHI mailing lists:
http://www.sigchi.org/connect/mailing-lists

ACM MM-INTEREST (ACM SIGMM)
mm-interest@listserv.acm.org

BCS HCI mailinglist:
http://www.bcs-hci.org.uk/mailinglist

15.6.2 Sample conference calendars

There are plenty of conference calendars around. A good tool is the "approaching deadline site":
http://www.interaction-design.org/calendar/approaching_deadlines.html

ACM Conference Calendar:
http://www.acm.org/conferences

BCS Conference Calendar:
http://www.bcs.org/server.php?show=nav.9231

Austrian Computer Society OCG Event Calendar
http://kalender.ocg.at

15.6.3 Samples of Interdisciplinary Conferences

There are many conferences, here just a small selection, see also
http://hci4all.at/projects4students.html
In the following order: <Name>; <Interval>; <Acronym>; <Main Organization>; <Founding year>; <Approximate Number of Participants (to estimate the size of the conference)>; <Usual Deadline>; <Usual Date>; <URL to Website>.

1) International Conference on Human–Computer Interaction;
bi-annually (odd years, next: 2011); HCI International; HCII, 1985, 2500; October, 15; July, 15-20; http://www.hci-international.org

2) Conference on Human Factors in Computing Systems; annually; CHI; ACM; 1982; 2500; September, 24, April 10-15; http://www.chi2011.org

3) International Joint Conference on e-Business and Telecommunications; annually; ICE-B; Institute for Systems and Technologies of Information, Control and Communication, INSTIC, 2005; 300; April, 22; July, 25-30; http://www.ice-b.icete.org

4) Human-Computer Interaction; annually; HCI; 1978; BCS – British Computer Society; 250; March, 19; September 1-5; http://www.hci2010.org

5) Usability Conference of the Austrian Computer Society; annually; USAB; 2005; Austrian Computer Society OCG; 200; June, 15; November, 2-4; http://usab-symposium.uni-klu.ac.at

6) IFIP TC13 Conference on Human-Computer Interaction; bi-annually; INTERACT; 1985; International Federation of Information Processing IFIP; 500; January, 10; September 5-9; http://www.interact2011.org

7) International Conference on Computers Helping People with Special Needs; bi-annually; ICCHP; 1982; Linz University, Austrian Computer Society; 500; February, 11; July, 10-15; http://www.icchp.org

8) International Conference on Knowledge Management and Knowledge Technologies; annually; iKNOW; 2000; Graz University of Technology, KNOW-Center; 500; April, 20; September 1-3; http://i-know.tugraz.at

16 Target: Journals

Excellent work can be the basis for a "real" scientific contribution amongst a conference, symposium or workshop. However, the Mercedes a solid archival journal contribution.

16.1 What is a Journal

These are peer-reviewed, archival, scholarly professional and periodical issues of publications. The review process usually is much harder than for a conference and takes sometimes a very long time: Usual turn-over times are up to 2 years and longer.

16.2 How to submit a paper for a journal

If you think your work is ready for submission, look for the most appropriate target, i.e. where does your paper fit best. For this you should know the most important journals in your area – exactly those which you read already regularly and where you used articles for your related work. Consequently, you know the usual length, style, difficulty etc. and can determine if you submit it or not. Under all circumstances read the author instructions.

16.3 Author instructions

They provide you the requested details about a submission, i.e. the formal criteria, what to send (manuscript, letter of the corresponding author, figures separately, summary separately, author details separately, etc.) and where to send (e.g. submitting via e-mail or uploading via a journal management tool, e.g. manuscript central).

The instructions can be found on the websites of the journals. Look also for current Call for Papers. It is always good to contact the responsible editor-in-chief.

16.4 Sample journals

To date approximately 9000 journals are listed in the SCI, here only some relevant journals, without priority, not sorted, in the following order: <Full title of the Journal>; <JCR [20] Abbreviation>; <Impact Factor 2009>; < Citations[21]>; <Issues per Year[22]>; <Website>.

1) Communications of the ACM; COMMUN ACM; 2,646; 12617; 12; http://cacm.acm.org

2) IEEE Software; IEEE SOFTWARE; 2,732; 2713; 06; http://www.computer.org/portal/web/software/home

3) IEEE Computer; IEEE COMPUTER; 2,591; 3133; 12; http://www.computer.org/portal/web/computer

4) International Journal of Medical Informatics; INT J MED INFORM; 2,000; 1100; 12; http://www.sciencedirect.com/science/journal/13865056

5) Journal of Systems and Software; J SYST SOFTWARE; 1,312; 1570; 15; http://www.sciencedirect.com/science/journal/01641212

6) Online Information Review; ONLINE INFORM REV; 1,103; 268; 06; http://www.emeraldinsight.com/products/journals

---

[20] The abbreviated title used in Journal Citation Reports

[21] The total number of citations to the journal in the respective JCR year

[22] I/Y = Issues/Year = infers a crude estimation about the turn-over time

7) Information and Software Technology; INFORM SOFTWARE TECH; 1,200; 1045; 14;
http://www.sciencedirect.com/science/journal/09505849

8) Multimedia Tools and Applications; MULTIMED TOOLS APPL; 0,704; 308; 06;
http://www.springerlink.com/content/1380-7501

9) Software Practice and Experience; SOFTWARE PRACT EXP; 0,406; 14;
http://onlinelibrary.wiley.com/journal/10.1002/%28ISSN%291097-024X

10) Empirical Software Engineering; EMPIR SOFTW ENG; 1,091; 309; 4;
http://www.springer.com/computer/swe/journal/10664

11) Information & Management; INFORM MANAGE; 2,358; 2919; 12;
http://www.sciencedirect.com/science/journal/03787206

12) Information Processing and Management; INFORM PROCESS MANAG; 1,852; 2003; 6;
http://www.sciencedirect.com/science/journal/03064573

For comparison:

Science; SCIENCE, 28,10; 409290; 51;
http://www.sciencemag.org

New England Journal of Medicine; NEW ENGL J MED; 50,017; 205750; 52; http://www.nejm.org

17 Target: Research Grants

17.1 Money

In fact money is a necessary factor for all type of research at all levels, i.e. to finance manpower, equipment, materials, mobility, workshops, travels, etc.,

Here you find some information about the most important research grant possibilities, from a local (Austria) point of view. Clickable links, see http://hci4all.at/projects4students.html

Be persistent! Look through all the possible sources systematically.

17.2 Mobility

From the early beginning students are encouraged to participate in exchange programs or just spend a short time at an international institution, there are several funding possibilities:

Mobility Local. Outgoing Short Travel Fund from TU Graz, consult the International Relations and Mobility Department, see: http://portal.tugraz.at/portal/page/portal/Internationale_Beziehung en/Outgoings/KUWI

Mobility Regional. The "Abteilung 3 Wissenschaft und Forschung" of the Styrian Government, supports academics in active participation (having a paper at a conference) and mobility, however only if you are employed to an academic unit, consult: http://www.verwaltung.steiermark.at/cms/beitrag/10001095/9654

Mobility National. The Austrian Research Community (Österreichische Forschungs Gemeinschaft (ÖFG), offers some opportunities, see: http://www.oefg.at/text/ik.htm

Mobility European. In the Seventh Framework Programme of the European Union, the Marie-Curie Actions have been reinforced in the so-called People Programme. Entirely dedicated to human resources in research, this programme has a budget of 4,7 billion EUR over a seven year period until 2013. Have a closer look at:
http://cordis.europa.eu/fp7/people/home_en.html

Mobility European. Another program is ERASMUS, see:
http://eacea.ec.europa.eu/llp/erasmus/erasmus_en.php

Life Long Learning Programme.
http://ec.europa.eu/education/llp/doc1943_en.htm

17.3 Student scholarships

Scholarship. First of all check whether you can apply for a scholarship (Stipendium). There is a very useful tool, the OEH[23]-Stipendienrechner, see:
http://www.oeh.ac.at/quicklinks/oeh_stipendienrechner

Personal Grants. A good start also is to look for personal grants:
http://www.grants.at

Educational Grants Austria. Bildungsförderungen in Österreich
http://www.berufsinfo.at/bildungsfoerderung

Förderkompass Austria. BMVIT
http://www.foerderkompass.at

---

[23] ÖH = Austrian Students Union, see: http://www.oeh.ac.at

17.4 Research Funding

Styrian Business Promotion Agency. The Steirische Wirtschaftsfoerderung (SFG) aims to contribute to the strengthening and growth of the Styrian economy – especially towards the exchange between Academics and Industry:
http://www.sfg.at/cms/1312/English

Grant Database of the Austrian Federal Economic Chamber. Foerderdatenbank der Wirtschaftskammer Österreich:
http://portal.wko.at/wk/foe_suche.wk?sbid=190&ttid=21&dstid=0

Austrian FFG Grant Assistant. The FFG Förderassistent is provided by the Austrian Research Promotion Agency (FFG) and is the national funding institution for applied industrial research in Austria, and is a very effective tool:
http://www.ffg.at/content.php?cid=307

FIT IT Program. This focuses on research in information and communication technology and promotes visionary and interdisciplinary projects, which lead to significant technological innovations and simultaneously open up new application areas (future markets). Target groups are companies and research institutions, that contribute to the latest technical developments.
http://www.ffg.at/content.php?cid=101

Classical Standalone FWF-Project. Funding of individual research in the area of non-profit oriented scientific research
http://www.fwf.ac.at/en/projects/stand-alone_projects.html

Slovenian Research Agency [ARRS]. Slovenia is a border country in the south of Austria, e.g. Graz and Maribor are only 45 minutes by car:

http://www.arrs.gov.si/en/dobrodoslica.asp

German Research Agency. The „Deutsche Forschungs-gemeinschaft (DFG)" is the central, self-governing and largest research funding organisation in Germany and promotes all fields of science and the humanities.
http://www.dfg.de/en/index.jsp

German Research Data base. The „Deutsche Förder-datenbank" is a very useful tool to get a good overview:
http://www.foerderdatenbank.de

European Research Information. The CORDIS portal is *the* gateway to European research and development:
http://cordis.europa.eu/home_en.html

European Project Partner Search. The CORDIS Partners Service is a free on-line tool to help organizations locate suitable partners for both EU funded and/or private collaboration:
http://cordis.europa.eu/partners-service/search_en.html

UK Wellcome Trust. This is a global charity dedicated to support improvements in human health:
http://www.wellcome.ac.uk

US National Science Foundation. The NSF is an independent federal agency to promote the progress of science with an annual budget of 7 Billion USD (2010). In many fields such as mathematics, computer science and the social sciences, NSF is the major source of federal backing:
http://www.nsf.gov

US National Institute of Health. The NIH is the nation's medical research agency, making important medical discoveries that improve health and save lives.
http://www.nih.gov

World Health Organization. The WHO is the directing and coordinating authority for health within the United Nations system and shapes research agendas, norms and standards, technical support to countries and monitoring and assessing health trends:
http://www.who.int/en

17.5 How to write a project proposal

A project proposal is very similar to a paper. As a paper it will be peer reviewed. On the basis of the reviewers outcome your proposal will be accepted or declined, however, sometimes it is just too less money available, consequently sometimes even excellent proposals get rejected.

Before you start, you should careful think about this four issues:

VISION – Where do you want to go (e.g. your objectives)?

MISSION – Why do you want to do it (e.g. your convictions)?

POLICY – How do you achieve your Vision (e.g. your possibilities)?

STRATEGY – What instruments do you use (your plans, e.g. project funding targets, etc.)

All proposals follow the – more or less – same logical and formal structure:

Title and Acronym. The Title must be convincing and the acronym must be catchy.

Abstract. It is the most important part and must be absolutely convincing. Note that an expert reader, working in this field for many years, will evaluate it. The abstract can be in unstructured or structured form but in both cases must contain the same parts.

a) Introduction and motivation:
<clearly state what the core problem is and why there is a need for a research project, the abstract is the most important part, it must be absolutely convincing >

b) Objectives: This project will ...
<clearly state what the project will do and what the benefit is and why it should be funded>

c) Methods:
<which methods will be used in this project>

d) Expected Results:
<What are the main expected outcomes of this project, again: Why should somebody release money for this project, what is the unique proposition point>

Keywords: Human–Computer Interaction, Usability Research, (up to five keywords) ...

OESTAT Topics < exactly 4 topics and the percents relevant>:

Table of content

Abbreviations and Acronyms

Content

1. Introduction and motivation for research

<Why is this research necessary? Why should it be done? What is the main reason for this?>

2. Background and Related Work

The background constitutes the necessary theories, concepts and fundamentals; the related work constitutes current work that relates to the topic – state of the art – body of knowledge, it is the work of other colleagues, most obvious the reviewers of the project proposals. It is essential nothing to ignore or forget; if a potential reviewer is referenced the changes raises ;-)
Basically, the related work includes the shoulders were we stand and which we should know, this includes all state-of-the art papers (journals and conferences) and – most important – patents!

< what is the work we are building on ? These are the shoulders were we stand and which we should know, this includes all state-of-the art papers (journals and conferences) and patents >

3. Project Objectives

Coarsely describe the MAIN research targets and point to the detailed work plan and research agenda in section 5. Here just provide convincing what the main QUESTIONS are and how you address them and what you expect to find.
This should be just **convincing** (e.g. the reviewer must see that you are not only know your field, that you want to go beyond state of the art and are motivated, but also that you are able to achieve your goals).

4. Methods and Materials

Describe the systems, equipment, development kits etc. which will be used during this project, however, be aware that it is a research project so describe the methods which will be applied in the research during this project (e.g. Heuristic Evaluation, Cognitive Walkthrough, Action Analysis; Thinking aloud, Field Observation, Questionnaires; Task Analysis; Video Analysis; Contextual Inquiry; Verbal Protocols; Interviews; Concurrent Ethnography; Rapid Ethnography; Rapid Prototyping, Co-Discovery Method; Biological Usability Testing; EEG Methods, EOG Methods, Formal Methods (Petri Nets, Markov Models, etc.).

5 Research agenda (incl. Gantt-Chart)

5.1 Work package 1: <WP Title>

< as many work packages as are needed>

The most important part of a grant application is a convincing presentation of work packages with clear inputs, processes and outputs.

The whole project is divided into <number> Workpackages (WPs) having various duration (see Gantt-Chart on page <pagenumber>). Some of the tasks can be done concurrently, others sequentially, with some overlap. In the areas, where the project goals are to ambitious, where not all and every research question can be addressed, it shall be emphasized that this parts will serve as pilot studies with the central aim of providing a well-grounded prototype development which can be used for further research.

WP Number	XX	Duration: x months	PM: x
WP Title	<A concise title of the work package>		
Motivation for WP	<Give a justification of why this WP is necessary and important>		
WP Objectives	<Provide the objectives, goals and aims of this WP>		
Related Work: Main Publications	<Describe at least three main related publications, patents>		
Research Questions	<Define the most important research questions>		
Methods and Materials	<Describe the main methods and the material used within this WP>		
Expected Outcomes: Deliverables	<Provide a list of expected outcomes, e.g. Technical Report; Contribution to conference X; Submission to journal Y; Mock-Up; Conceptual model; Proof of Concept; Prototype; Patent>		

Figure 17: A typical Workpackage Sheet

6   Project Cost Calculation

6.1   Table of Expenses

6.2   Details to costs of requested materials

6.3   Details to costs of requested travel expenses

6.4   Details to costs of planned workshops

7   Information on the Research Institution (Infrastructure)

Example:

The Medical University of Graz (MUG) comprises 40 clinical and non-clinical institutions. It is closely associated with a top quality hospital – one of the largest in Europe – offering essentially all fields of medicine. There are about 700 academics (among them 80 university professors) and more than 300 other personnel. More than 4000 students pursue their studies at the university, thus many of the academics are regularly involved in teaching. MUG is within the core of a network of 22 general hospitals of the province Styria (population approx. 1.200.000 people). There are also good connections to residential home for the older people. The Research Unit Human-Computer Interaction for Medicine and Health "HCI4MED" of the Institute for Medical Informatics, Statistics and Documentation (IMI) of the Medical University of Graz, integrates – in addition to the necessary technological aspects – human-centred, cognitive aspects of information processing. The RU HCI4MED has established cooperation's to the Department of Psychology (Cognitive Science Section) of Graz University and the Department of Information Systems and Computer Media (IICM), thereby having access to an large method pool (EEG, Eyetracking, EOG, observation equipment, etc.). The Research Unit is also internationally well connected. The Research Unit HCI4MED has interdisciplinary experience in EU programs and national research programs and experience in supervision of PhD students. The MUG has an PhD school for the research area: sustainable health.

8   Team

Example:
The following team members contribute to this project
(short 100-words bio):

Assoc.Prof. Dr. Andreas Holzinger is head of the RU HCI4MED, Associate Professor for Applied Informatics at Graz University of Technology and elected chair of the Workgroup Human–Computer Interaction and Usability Engineering (HCI&UE) of the Austrian Computer Society and leader and founder of the national Special Interest Groups HCI4MED and HCI4EDU. He is Austrian representative in the Technical Committee TC 13 HCI of the International Federation of Information Processing (IFIP). He was visiting Professor in Berlin, Innsbruck, Vienna and London. To date 259 publications and 177 lectures/talks (August 2010). More information: http://user.meduni-graz.at/andreas.holzinger.

< bios ... 100 words each >

9   Dissemination Strategy

<What conferences do you want to target? In which journals would you like to publish your results?

10   References

<finally, the literature used in the proposal>

The proposal should within 20 pages maximum include everything, which a reviewer needs for judgement.

18   Further Reading

A commented literature list ("kommentierte Literaturliste") is highly recommendable for your work, too. The idea is to write a few sentences on the **core essence** of the content and to provide some strengths and weaknesses. Here only a few examples:

Day, Robert A.: How to Write and Publish a Scientific Paper
1998, 6th Edition. Westport (CT): Oryx Press. 320 pp. EUR 23,-
A classical reader from an university professor of English who taught scientific and technical writing and editing.
+ Strengths: Nice to read, interesting, seen from a relatively subject-neutral viewpoint; including e.g. chapter 29: How to present a paper orally, p.182; chapter 32: Use and Misuse of English, p. 200;
– Weaknesses: a very general, verbose introduction to the art of scientific writing for beginners and not specifically for engineering; it is a reader, not a checklist, consequently you need some time for this book.

Chalmers, Alan F.: What is this thing called Science?
1999, 3rd Edition. Berkshire (UK), Open University Press. 288 pp. EUR 29,90,-
A classical reader from an professor of History and Philosophy of Science about the basics of Science. Chapter 12 contains an introduction into the Bayesian approach. There is also a German Translation "Wege der Wege der Wissenschaft: Einführung in die Wissenschaftstheorie", which has an interesting appendix, i.e. a selection of books on the Theory of Science of various disciplines.
+ Strengths: Interesting and nice to read. German translation contains a very good appendix on different subjects.
– Weaknesses: Very general and very exhaustive, verbose, definitely will need some time to read, can lead astray;

Zinser, W.: On Writing Well
2006, 30th Edition. New York: Harper Collins. 336 pp. EUR 12,-
Written by a reporter, this book is generally on writing style and includes principles, methods, forms and attitudes.
+ Strengths: Excellent advice on writing style.
− Weaknesses: Very general, not specifically intended for computer scientists; covers only language style aspects.

Lazar, J., Feng, J.H., Hochheiser, H.: Research Methods in Human-Computer Interaction
2010, 1st Edition. Chichester (UK): Wiley, 426pp. EUR 59,60
Written by long-time experts in the field, this is a must read for any HCI professional and one of the best resources .
+ Strengths: Excellent resource, detailed information but still easy to read, provides excellent theoretical background.
− Weaknesses: Very elaborated, nearly too much for a standard course, needs much time to read, focused only on research.

Rubin, J., Chisnell, D.: Handbook of Usability Testing.
2008, 2nd Edition. Indianapolis: Wiley, 348 pp. EUR 44,60
Clear, step-by-step guidelines to help to test a product for usability.
+ Strengths: Very practical, simple, easy to read.
− Weaknesses: Far too less background theory, rather a cookbook, exhaustive on some details, lacking much other aspects.

Thimbley, H.: press on: Principles of Interaction Programming
2007, Cambridge (MA): MIT Press. 510pp. EUR 38,99
Written by a professor of Computer Science this book is convincing on the importance of HCI and usability. Must read.
+ Strengths: Deep, interesting, challenging.
− Weaknesses: Needs much time to read.

19 Glossary

ACM = Association of Computing Machinery, founded in 1947 as the first computer society in the world; http://www.acm.org

ANOVA = Analysis of Variance, to determine differences among the mean values (when the independent variables are nominal, dependent variable is usual an interval.

Confounding Variable = an unforeseen, unwanted variable that jeopardizes reliability and validity of a study outcome.

Correlation coefficent = measures the relationship between pairs of interval variables in a sample, from $r = -1.00$ to 0 (no correlation) to $r = +1.00$

External Validity = the extent to which the results of a study are generalizable or transferable.

Internal Validity = the rigor with which a study was conducted (e.g., the design, the care taken to conduct measurements, and decisions concerning what was and was not measured).

Qualitative Research = empirical research exploring relationships using textual, rather than quantitative data, e.g. case study, observation, ethnography; Results are not considered generalizable, but sometimes at least transferable.

Quantitative Research = empirical research exploring relationships using numeric data, e.g. surveys, quasi-experiments, experiments. Results should be generalized, although it is not always possible.

Randomization = allocating subjects to experimental and control groups.

Reliability = the extent to which a procedure yields the same result on repeated trials.

Significance Level = p-Value, type I error (alpha error), the fixed probability of wrongly rejecting the null hypothesis H0, if it is in fact true. It is chosen mostly to be $p < 0.05$ (that means, if H0 were to be rejected at the 5% significance level).

20 Index

Index

Index

Index

Index

21 References

Batista, P. D., Campiteli, M. G., Kinouchi, O. & Martinez, A. S. (2006) Is it possible to compare researchers with different scientific interests? *Scientometrics,* 68, 1, 179-189.

Blankenberger, S. & Vorberg, D. (1998), Die Auswahl statistischer Tests und Maße. Online available: http://web.fu-berlin.de/biometrie/PDFs/Entscheidungsbaum%20P oster.pdf, last access: 2009-08-11

Bloom, B. S. (1956) *Taxonomy of educational objectives, handbook 1: Cognitive domain.* New York, Longmans Green.

Bortz, J. & Döring, N. (2006) *Forschungmethoden und Evaluation für Human- und Sozialwissenschaftler. 4.Auflage.* Berlin, Heidelberg Springer.

Bulling, A., Roggen, D. & Troester, G. (2008). *It's in your eyes: towards context-awareness and mobile HCI using wearable EOG goggles.* Proceedings of the 10th international conference on Ubiquitous computing, Seoul (Korea), ACM, 84-93.

Cairns, P. & Cox, A. L. (Eds.) (2008) *Research Methods for Human-Computer Interaction,* Cambridge (UK), Cambridge University Press.

Card, S. K., Moran, T. P. & Newell, A. (1980) The keystroke-level model for user performance time with interactive systems. *Communications of the ACM,* 23, 7, 396-410.

Card, S. K., Moran, T. P. & Newell, A. (1983) *The psychology of Human-Computer Interaction.* Hillsdale (NJ), Erlbaum.

Carroll, J. M. (2002) Making use is more than a matter of task analysis. *Interacting with Computers,* 14, 5, 619-627.

Chalmers, A. F. (2009) *What is this thing called Science?* Berkshire (UK), Open University Press.

Christensen, L. B. (2001) *Experimental methodology.* Boston, London, Toronto et.al., Allyn and Bacon.

Christensen, L. B. (2006) *Experimental methodology. 10th Edition.* Boston, London, Toronto et.al., Allyn and Bacon.

Dalgaard, P. (2002) *Introductory Statistics with R.* Berlin, Springer.

DeMarco, T. (1982) *Controlling software projects. Management, measurement & estimation. Foreword by Barry W. Boehm* Englewood Cliffs (NJ), Yourdon Press.

Deming, W. E. (1994) *The new economics.* Cambridge (MA), MIT Press.

Garfield, E. (1972) Citation Analysis as a Tool in Journal Evaluation - Journals Can Be Ranked by Frequency and Impact of Citations for Science Policy Studies. *Science,* 178, 4060, 471-479.

Garfield, E. (1989) The English-Language - the Lingua Franca of International Science. *Scientist,* 3, 10, 12-12.

Goh, J. W. P., Quek, C. J. & Lee, O. K. (2010) An Investigation of Students' Perceptions of Learning Benefits of Weblogs in an East Asian Context: A Rasch Analysis. *Educational Technology & Society,* 13, 2, 90-101.

Harper, R., Rodden, T., Rogers, Y. & Sellen, A. (2008) *Being Human: Human-Computer Interaction in the Year 2020.* Cambridge, Microsoft Research.

Hirsch, J. E. (2005) An index to quantify an individual's scientific research output. *Proceedings of the National Academy of Sciences of the United States of America,* 102, 46, 16569-16572.

Holzinger, A. (2004) Application of Rapid Prototyping to the User Interface Development for a Virtual Medical Campus. *IEEE Software,* 21, 1, 92-99.

Holzinger, A. (2005) Usability Engineering for Software Developers. *Communications of the ACM,* 48, 1, 71-74.

Holzinger, A., Kickmeier-Rust, M. & Albert, D. (2008) Dynamic Media in Computer Science Education; Content Complexity and Learning Performance: Is Less More? *Educational Technology & Society,* 11, 1, 279-290.

Hornback, E. R. (1996) Method and System for detecting the proper functioning of an ABS control unit utilizing dual programmed microprocessors. EP0771280.

Jakob, D. (2008) Englisch als globale Wissenschaftssprache. *Akademische Blätter Online: Zeitschrift des Verbandes der Vereine Deutscher Studenten,* 2.

Lazar, J., Feng, J. H. & Hochheiser, H. (2010) *Research Methods in Human-Computer Interaction.* Chichester (UK), Wiley.

Lewis, C. & Wharton, C. (1997) Cognitive Walkthroughs. In: Helander, M. (Ed.) *Handbook of Human-Computer Interaction. Second Edition.* Amsterdam, Elsevier, 717-732.

Mandryk, R. L., Inkpen, K. M. & Calvert, T. W. (2006) Using psychophysiological techniques to measure user experience with entertainment technologies. *Behaviour & Information Technology,* 25, 2, 141-158.

Manstead, A. S. R. & Semin, G. R. (1992) Methoden der Sozialpsychologie: Von der Vorstellung zur Handlung. In: Stroebe, W., Hewstone, M., Codol, J.-P. & Stephenson, G. M. (Eds.) *Sozialpsychologie. Eine Einführung.* Heidelberg, Berlin, New York, Springer.

Montgomery, D. C. (2008) *Design and Analysis of Experiments, 6th Edition.* New York, John Wiley.

Nielsen, J. (1994) *Usability Engineering.* San Francisco, Morgan Kaufmann.

Nielsen, J. & Mack, R. L. (Eds.) (1994) *Usability Inspection Methods,* New York, Wiley.

Poh, M. Z., Swenson, N. C. & Picard, R. W. (2010) A Wearable Sensor for Unobtrusive, Long-Term Assessment of Electrodermal Activity. *Ieee Transactions on Biomedical Engineering,* 57, 5, 1243-1252.

Popper, K. (2005) *Logik der Forschung.* Tübingen, Mohr.

Rubin, J. & Chisnell, D. (2008) *Handbook of Usability Testing. How to Plan, Design, and Conduct Effective Tests. Second Edition.* Indianapolis (IN), Wiley.

Sarris, V. (1992) *Methodologische Grundlagen der Experimentalpsychologie. Band 2: Versuchsplanung und Stadien des psychologischen Experiments. : .* München, Reinhardt.

Scholtes, P. R. (1999) The new competencies of leadership. *Total Quality Management,* 10, 4-5, S704-S710.

Sears, A. L. (1997) Heuristic walkthroughs: Finding problems without the noise. *International Journal of Human-Computer Interaction,* 9, 3, 213-234.

Shewhart, W. A. (1958) Nature and Origin of Standards of Quality. *Bell System Technical Journal,* 37, 1, 1-22.

Stepanovich, P. L. (2004) Using system dynamics to illustrate Deming's System of Profound Knowledge.

Total Quality Management & Business Excellence, 15, 3, 379-389.

Stevens, S. S. (1946) On the theory of scales of measurement. *Science,* 103, 677-680.

Stickel, C., Ebner, M., Steinbach-Nordmann, S., Searle, G. & Holzinger, A. (2009) Emotion Detection: Application of the Valence Arousal Space for Rapid Biological Usability Testing to Enhance Universal Access. In: Stephanidis, C. (Ed.) *Universal Access in HCI, Part I, HCII 2009, Lecture Notes in Computer Science (LNCS 5614).* Berlin, Heidelberg, New York, Springer, 615-624.

Stickel, C., Fink, J. & Holzinger, A. (2007) Enhancing Universal Access – EEG based Learnability Assessment. In: Stephanidis, C. (Ed.) *Universal Access to Applications and Services. Lecture Notes in Computer Science (LNCS 4556).* Berlin, Heidelberg, New York, Springer, 813-822.

Thimbleby, H. (2007) *press on: Principles onf Interaction Programming.* Cambridge (MA), MIT Press.

Velleman, P. F. & Wilkinson, L. (1993) Nominal, Ordinal, Interval, and Ratio Typologies Are Misleading. *American Statistician,* 47, 1, 65-72.

Wengelin, A., Torrance, M., Holmqvist, K., Simpson, S., Galbraith, D., Johansson, V. & Johansson, R. (2009) Combined eyetracking and keystroke-logging methods for studying cognitive processes in text production. *Behavior Research Methods,* 41, 2, 337-351.

Wickens, C., Lee, J., Liu, Y. & Gordon-Becker, S. (2004) *Introduction to Human Factors Engineering: Second Edition.* Upper Saddle River (NJ), Prentice-Hall.

Wu, J. & Hamada, M. (2000) *Experiments: Planning, Analysis and Parameter Design Optimization* New York, John Wiley

Wynn, E. (2001) Some informal thoughts about reviewing as a social process. *Journal of Systems and Software,* 59, 2, 115-117.

Herstellung und Verlag:
Books on Demand GmbH, Norderstedt
ISBN 978-3-8423-2457-2

www.ingramcontent.com/pod-product-compliance
Lightning Source LLC
LaVergne TN
LVHW052301060326
832902LV00021B/3664